HEARING FROM
GOD

5 Steps to Knowing His Will for Your Life

DAVID STINE

HOWARD BOOKS

New York   London   Toronto   Sydney   New Delhi

HOWARD
BOOKS

HOWARD BOOKS
An Imprint of Simon & Schuster, Inc.
1230 Avenue of the Americas
New York, NY 10020

First Howard Books trade paperback edition October 2018

HOWARD and colophon are trademarks of Simon & Schuster, Inc.

For information about special discounts for bulk purchases,
please contact Simon & Schuster Special Sales at 1-866-506-1949
or business@simonandschuster.com.

The Simon & Schuster Speakers Bureau can bring authors to your live event.
For more information or to book an event, contact the Simon & Schuster Speakers Bureau
at 1-866-248-3049 or visit our website at www.simonspeakers.com.

Interior design by Davina Mock-Maniscalco

Manufactured in the United States of America

10 9 8 7 6 5 4 3 2 1

Library of Congress Cataloging-in-Publication Data

Names: Stine, David Isaac, author.
Title: Hearing from God: 5 steps to knowing His will for your life / David Stine.
Description: First [edition]. | Nashville : Howard Books, 2017. |
Includes bibliographical references.
Identifiers: LCCN 2016010292| ISBN 9781501147326 (hardcover) |
ISBN 9781501147791 (tradepaper) | ISBN 9781501147333 (ebook)
Subjects: LCSH: Prayer—Christianity. | Spirituality—Christianity. |
Spiritual life—Christianity. | God (Christianity)—Will. |
Listening—Religious aspects—Christianity. | Devotional literature.
Classification: LCC BV215 .S8175 2017 | DDC 248.4—dc23
LC record available at https://lccn.loc.gov/2016010292

ISBN 978-1-5011-4732-6
ISBN 978-1-5011-4779-1 (pbk)
ISBN 978-1-5011-4733-3 (ebook)

Praise for *Hearing from God*

"David Stine's work and pastoral sensitivities flavor this entire book and his grounding in God's Word provides its strong foundation and practical viability. Read it—and move forward toward a goal of learning the joys and blessing that transcends the trials and lessons life inevitably brings us all. You will be profited, your heart instructed, your mind sharpened, and your feet secured on your way as you listen to God's voice."

—**Jack W. Hayford,** chancellor of The King's University in Southlake, Texas;
pastor emeritus of The Church On The Way in Van Nuys, California;
and author of *Prayer Is Invading the Impossible*

"In a culture where there can be many competing 'voices' in our lives, the voice that carries the greatest weight can only come from God. God desires relational intimacy with all of us and this can only be cultivated by learning to listen and recognize His voice. David Stine has written a powerful and highly practical book that de-mystifies this process. This is a must-read for everyone!"

—**Stovall Weems,** Lead Pastor of Celebration Church in Jacksonville, Florida,
and author of *Living the God-First Life*

"Having had the privilege of knowing David and his wife personally for over twenty years, I can say that David Stine knows what it means to walk with God. His life is an example of someone who seeks the Lord with all of his heart. This book will help resurrect your walk with God as David uses his testimony and experiences to help you hear God's voice in your life. David is able to make complicated ideas understandable so that we can apply them to our lives. This book will help you to commit to seeking God first and everything else will be added to you.

—**Joe Champion,** Lead Pastor of Celebration Church in Austin, Texas,
and author of *Rocked: How to Respond When Life's Circumstances Rock You to Your Core*

"There is nothing more elemental to Christian pursuit or more essential to Christian living than hearing the voice of God. With equal parts good theology and good sense, David Stine's crack at this age-old question demystifies a cluttered subject and offers refreshing, practical help. With the intellectual honesty of a scientist, the care of a pastor, and the zeal of a man who lives this stuff, he helps us relate to a God who is both mystical and rational."

—**Rob Brendle**, Lead Pastor of Denver United Church in Denver, Colorado, and author of *In the Meantime: The Practice of Proactive Waiting*

"This book is not theory; it is the reality of a man who has tested it personally and vocationally, finding it both true and trustworthy. Reading Dr. David's personal milestone stories will give you hope and help to upgrade your own story of God's blueprint for your life and ministry. The good news is that the author makes the complicated simple without dumbing down the power and life change of 'a Word in season' in your own life.

Because I have watched this book work itself through the life of the author as my student, ministry staff, and now as an overseer for this esteemed and sought after church planter, I can attest to its truthfulness and fruitfulness. On the other side of this exciting read you will have a hunger and thirst for hearing and obeying our Abba Father, who calls you by name and leads you out into this courageous adventure of trusting His daily voice to you."

—**Dr. Joseph Umidi**, Interim Dean of Divinity and Executive Vice President of Regent University in Virginia Beach, Virginia, and author of *Transformational Coaching*

To My Grandfather

I watched you study your Bible, while I studied your life, and you made me want to know the God that you knew. You taught me about hearing the voice of God and, in many ways, inspired the journey that led to this book.
I can't wait to see you again.

Contents

Contents

Foreword

I n my time as a pastor, I've had countless individuals ask me how to make their spiritual lives more exciting. They want to know how they can have a more dynamic prayer life. They long for a two-way conversation with God rather than their one-sided presentation of a list of requests. These are good concerns, but this truth I share in response may be hard to swallow: if you are bored as a Christian, perhaps you are not actively following in the footsteps of Jesus.

You see, when we have an interactive prayer life and we follow Jesus' lead, irregular and spectacular things happen on a regular basis. *Hearing from God* contains incredible stories of what has happened in the life of my good friend and fellow pastor David Stine when God showed up on the scene. What I most appreciate about this book, though, is that David helps you learn how to hear God's voice for yourself so you can experience your own adventure with Him.

I have known David for over a decade, and he is a gifted leader, a humble servant, and someone who regularly hears from God. When I first met David, we immediately connected over our love for the Washington, D.C., area, as we have the incredible honor of pastoring in the same city. I know that, whenever we get together for dinner, I will hear about his latest experience following the voice of God. What he shares always awakens in me the desire for more "God encounters" in my own life and reminds me of the wisdom of following Him wherever He leads.

Learning to recognize God's voice has been an absolute game changer in my life. In fact, I can't think of a more important skill for a believer to develop than learning to hear God. If you have ever read any of my books, you may have noticed the common theme of reclaiming the adventure of pursuing God and going where His voice leads. Once you've tasted this, you are ruined for anything less.

As I have shared on my blog, the Holy Spirit speaks in lots of different dialects. He knows every language, including your own unique language. He knows what to say and how to say it. And He is always speaking—but do you recognize His voice? If you aren't listening, you won't hear it. If you aren't looking for God encounters, you won't see them. But if you open your ears and open your eyes, you will hear God's voice and see Him everywhere!

I recommend *Hearing from God* for God-followers who want to learn how to open their eyes and ears so that they, too, can see and hear God everywhere. I appreciate how simple David makes the practice of hearing from God. He gives you a step-by-step guide to position yourself to hear from Him and outlines a forty-day "experiment" in the back of the book so that you can practice everything he teaches. If you read this book and put its ideas into practice, not only will your relationship with God deepen, but I am confident that your ability to hear from Him more clearly and more consistently will grow exponentially!

Mark Batterson
Lead Pastor of National Community Church
and bestselling author of *The Circle Maker*

HEARING FROM
GOD

PART ONE

CONTACT

There is a great sci-fi movie that came out in 1997 called *Contact*. Based on a Carl Sagan novel by the same name, the movie follows the main character, Ellie Arroway, from childhood to her career as a research scientist with the SETI program (Search for Extraterrestrial Intelligence). The preteen Ellie—later Dr. Arroway—has an insatiable desire to make contact with the outside world. What starts as reaching outside of her childhood home through a CB radio develops into a life devoted to searching for life outside our solar system.

In the opening scenes of the movie, Ellie excitedly makes contact on her CB radio with someone in Florida, which leads to questions about the possibility of making contact with the different stars she views through her telescope. Eventually, as an adult, her search for contact from worlds beyond pays off, as she receives a series of communications from the distant star Vega.

One of the most gripping scenes takes place early in the movie after Ellie's father dies. In the midst of the tragedy, while family and friends are downstairs socializing after the funeral, Ellie is up in her bedroom, seated in front of the CB radio, attempting to make contact: "Dad, are you there? This is Ellie. Dad, are you there?"

I called this book *Hearing from God: 5 Steps to Knowing His Will for Your Life* because I believe, as humans, we all want to make contact with our Heavenly Father and hear and recognize His voice. We want to know what He has to say to us personally and know what His will is for us. Many of the world's religions are like Ellie's CB radio, where we call out to God as she called out to her father, "Are you there?" We all hope that perhaps we will get some kind of reply—an assurance that He exists and is somehow interested in our lives—even if it's only a scratchy, faint hum.

As believers I am convinced that God wants to make contact with us even more than we want to hear from Him. Instead of a faint, indistinguishable hum, He wants to speak clearly to His people. As Jeremiah 33:3 says, "Call to me and I will answer you and tell you great and unsearchable things you do not know."

God speaking to us is meant to be a normal part of our daily lives. Unfortunately, it can seem too time-consuming, inaccessible, inconceivable, or downright frustrating for many. According to a recent study by George Barna, more than 80 percent of Americans pray during a typical week, but only 38 percent are certain that Jesus talks back to them in a personal and relevant way, while an additional 21 percent are only somewhat certain that God speaks to them personally.[1]

The most common question I am asked as a pastor is, "How do I hear from God?" There is so much confusion, uncertainty, and ambiguity related to this subject, but I believe God wants to bring clarity so that conversational intimacy can be developed between Him and any believer. John 10:27 expresses that thought clearly: "My sheep listen to my voice; I know them, and they follow me." This is an invitation for all believers to listen to and hear God's voice.

The longer I have walked in a relationship with God, the more confident I have become that He wants to make contact, speaking specifically and frequently to each of us. So if He wants to speak and we want to hear, the million-dollar question is how do we position our lives to make that contact and hear clearly from God? As a pastor, I fully understand how difficult this can be, and there have been times in my life (which I will share in this book) where I missed God's voice in important ways. However, I have learned invaluable truths and practical applications that have absolutely revolutionized my walk with God and my ability to hear from Him. I have also found that the biggest hindrance to hearing from God is me—not God.

So many believers either do not believe they have enough significance, let alone a significant role to play, in hearing from God, or they don't understand what they can do to recognize His voice. Instead, they buy into the lie that God is not personal—He doesn't speak to them directly—or that there's something wrong with them that keeps them from making contact.

The reality for most believers is that they just need some coaching on how they can position themselves to hear from Him and on how to recognize His voice. There is a concept I call the ministry of Eli. Eli was High Priest in the Jewish temple and was instrumental in helping the young boy Samuel (who later became a prophet) recognize the voice of God speaking to him (1 Samuel 3:1–10). I want this book to become like the ministry of Eli to you. I have benefited greatly from being coached in this area by other pastors, mentors, and friends, and I am excited to share with you what I have learned along the way.

I am confident that as you put into practice what I teach in this book, you, too, will make contact and hear Him. If you already hear from God, I believe this book will help you grow in your ability to hear His voice even more clearly and become even more grounded in your relationship with Him. As new challenges arise where God is calling you to step out in faith, you will be more prepared because your ear is attuned to what He is saying and you can recall His faithfulness through previous challenges to give you confidence to step out again. You'll find that the more God speaks to you and guides you, the more you'll be faced with. The enemy will do his best to distract you as well. Because of this, you can never be too grounded in this process.

The Practical Science

Science has been described as God allowing man to discover the secret workings of His incredible creation. For Dr. Arroway, although the search was not based on a faith in God, it was based on discovering whatever was out there in the unknown universe. I believe God wants to help man discover not only the secret workings of His natural creation, but also the secret workings of His supernatural realm, including hearing His voice. The term practical science is defined as "the discipline of applying specific knowledge to practical problems." It is the synthesis of these two concepts that coveys the heart of this book.

Hearing from God is written to help believers discover and apply specific knowledge to the practical dilemma of wanting to hear clearly from God so that we can experience more depth in our relationship with Him. Although hearing from God cannot be reduced to an exact science in the typical connotation of the word, I believe there are specific action steps to take and important components we need to include in the formula of our lives to increase our propensity and frequency of hearing from Him. We live in the natural realm, but as believers we are also called to seek out the supernatural realm through a vibrant relationship with the living God. So how do we put this into practice?

The Scientific Method

Do you remember the scientific method from high school or college days? Since I am causing many of you to dig deep into the recesses of your mind, let me give you a little refresher. For those of you who are not science minded, please hang in there with me. I promise this will be simple and even intriguing.

The scientific method is a body of techniques for investigating phenomena, acquiring knowledge, or correcting and integrating previous knowledge. It includes the following six steps:

- ✦ **Step One:** Ask a Question
- ✦ **Step Two:** Do Background Research
- ✦ **Step Three:** Construct a Hypothesis
- ✦ **Step Four:** Test Your Hypothesis by Doing an Experiment

+ **Step Five:** Analyze Your Data and Draw a Conclusion

+ **Step Six:** Communicate Your Results

Although it is not a perfect correlation, when we apply the scientific method to hearing the voice of God, we come up with the following:

We ask God a question or questions, creating space and time in our lives to hear from Him (Step One).

We do background research, taking our question(s) and researching what the Word of God, the Bible, says about the topic (Step Two).

Listening for His voice and researching the Word of God should lead us to a hypothesis of what we believe God is speaking to us (Step Three).

We share what we believe God is speaking to us with trusted friends or counselors—testing to see if they confirm what we are hearing (Step Four).

We analyze what we have heard through His voice, His Word, His counsel through others, and see if our conclusion is confirmed by His peace (Step Five).

Finally, we tell others of what we have learned through this process and of what God has done in our lives (Step Six).

The Experiment

God invites each one of us to know His thoughts. Amos 3:7 says, "Surely the Lord God does nothing, unless He reveals His secret to His servants."[2] God wants to reveal His secrets to us, but we must seek Him. So, as you read through the chapters of this book, I invite you to participate in an experiment. A scientific supernatural experiment of sorts, which I am confident will help you grow exponentially in being able to hear and discern God's voice.

My challenge to you is to spend thirty minutes a day with God for forty days, intentionally positioning yourself to hear from Him. Thirty minutes is a good starting point, and I believe that as you begin to encounter God in prayer and His Word, your thirty minutes will soon turn into forty minutes or more. Thirty minutes a day of prayer, study, and allowing God's Word to bring transformation can lead to a radically changed life.

There is detailed guidance on how to position yourself to hear from God in part 3 of this book ("The Experiment—a 40-Day Guide to Hearing God's Voice"). To help you effectively spend your thirty minutes with God and increase your receptivity to hear from—and make contact with—Him, I unpack the five-step process I recommend for your devotional time:

+ **Step One:** Pick a Time and a Place to Meet with God

+ **Step Two:** Be Still and Worship

+ **Step Three:** Read and Pray

+ **Step Four:** Listen and Write

+ **Step Five:** Share and Obey

The "40-Day Challenge" includes forty daily Bible passages to study, a format to follow to help you in your time with Him, and space to journal and record what you are learning and hearing.

The theologian Frank Laubach stated, "Before a scientist tries an experiment, he must have faith in the work of those who already have reported success."[3] This book is a combination of what I have learned from walking with God, listening to Him, and gleaning from the wisdom and experience of others who have gone before me.

I believe that this book could change your life, but it won't happen without an intentional investment on your part. Will you say yes and commit to the experiment of spending thirty minutes a day, for forty days, seeking Him? As you take this step toward God and position yourself to hear from Him, He will come. Just as He said to the Israelites in Exodus 29:42, "I will meet with you and speak with you."[4] Get ready!

The Science-Loving, Want-To-Be Inventor

As a child, I was one of those quintessential science-loving, want-to-be inventors that wanted to compete in every science fair and had a certain obsession with creating something I could patent. My dream vacation was a trip to the Smithsonian Air and Space and Natural Science Museum in Washington, D.C. It was there that I felt like I found my people and realized I was not alone in my passion to discover.

That trip was a catalyst that fueled my desire to explore and discover. If I was going to be the next Einstein or Edison, I figured I'd better start learning to split atoms and create something that would revolutionize society. Okay, maybe not splitting atoms, but I felt inspired to dive headfirst into the world of science.

During those elementary years, it probably did not help my social status that I spent my free time reading science books and dreaming up what my next invention would be. I don't like to brag, but I will tell you that I entered six different science fairs and came home with more than my fair share of prizes. In fact, one year I won first prize in the school and an honorable mention in the regionals.

As a junior "mad scientist," I had one experiment go wrong . . . very wrong. It all started innocently enough on Christmas morning of my sixth grade year when I received the best present EVER. To me, it was the magnum opus of all Christmas gifts: my very own genuine chemistry set. Other boys my age were asking for autographed footballs, a new leather bomber jacket, or cassette tapes of Guns N' Roses, but who would want such frivolous items when you could have beakers and potent chemicals to mix together?

Upon receipt of the gift, I rushed upstairs to my room that was perfectly sequestered from the rest of the house to mix up some concoctions without any interruptions from my parents. The chemistry set came with a plethora of different chemicals, different-sized beakers, and an instruction book.

As I was the type of kid who never did anything by the book, I think it is fair to say that the instruction manual was probably never even opened. I mean who needs instruction manuals when you have chemicals, beakers, and a mad-scientist mind?

In the confines of my private laboratory (aka my bathroom), I began to mix different chemicals together. Each time I watched with awe and excitement, wondering what would happen next. Sometimes the different concoctions would voraciously bubble out of the beaker, and other times they would change colors right before my eyes, but nothing had prepared me for the concoction that accidentally turned my beaker into a flying rocket.

I am still not quite sure what I mixed together or why it suddenly turned explosive. All I remember is pouring in the last chemical and the beaker shooting out of my hand and hitting the ceiling. To my horror, I noticed a burning smell and an atrocious stain discoloring the ceiling. I somehow managed to avoid ever telling my parents, because later that same year they decided to have the bathroom painted a different color and the painters painted over the stain without my parents ever seeing. (Sorry. If you are reading this, Mom and Dad . . . please forgive me). Sometime later, after we had moved out of that house, it burned down. I couldn't help wondering if there was a connection to the chemicals on the ceiling from my science experiment gone awry.

Obviously, I can't say all my experiments were successful, but my obsession with science, and discovering why and how things in the natural world worked, continued for the rest of my middle school years. I was a committed explorer of the natural world until I had my first encounter with the supernatural on what was to be my, well, my deathbed.

The Vision, The Word, and The Healing

I will never forget the day I was diagnosed with terminal cancer. As a fifteen-year-old given only six weeks to live, I was petrified, confused, and in disbelief all at the same time. It was a game-changing moment in my life.

The first sign of sickness came during a tennis match at age fourteen. All of a sudden, in the middle of the match, I doubled over in pain and began regurgitating a water-like substance. I visited a myriad of doctors over the next year who tried to find a diagnosis for the painful symptoms I was experiencing. The doctors were baffled as to the cause, but the frequency of the incidents continued to increase until they were happening daily, even sometimes hourly, by the time I turned fifteen.

By this point, I had dropped in weight from 165 pounds to 110, and although we did not know what was wrong with me, we knew it was serious. At the age when most boys are thinking about school dances, sports, and learning to drive, I entered The Ochsner Medical Center in New Orleans for two weeks of intense tests and an examination by a panel of at least twenty different doctors.

After a series of tests—including a liver biopsy, a bone marrow test, and a spinal tap—I was diagnosed with a form of leukemia called eosinophilia, a condition that develops when the bone marrow makes too many eosinophils (a type of white blood cell). The doctors said there was nothing they could do and planned to send me home with a life expectancy of six weeks. The day before I was supposed to leave the hospital, the doctors took one more bone marrow test and a spinal tap, as I lay in the hospital bed in a state of devastation and disbelief over the prognosis I had received.

Sometime during that day my grandfather, who had been like a second father to me, called the hospital to speak with me. My grandfather was a man whom I deeply respected and loved. As a young boy I spent countless hours with him, visiting his house almost every day, where he helped me with my science experiments and building projects, speaking words of encouragement to me as a mentor.

In his call, Grandfather told me about a vision the Lord had given him where he saw me going up to heaven sickly in a hospital bed and then coming back down from the clouds healthy and dressed in normal clothes. My grandfather spoke with a humble confidence, "You are going to be healed. The Lord told me in prayer."

Although I was not walking with the Lord yet, I immediately clung to those words. My grandfather's words had weight, and what he spoke to me over the phone that afternoon became a source of hope in one of my darkest hours.

Not long after my grandfather shared his vision, as I lay there alone in my hospital bed, I realized that my previous symptoms had dissipated. The vomiting that had occurred like clockwork almost every fifteen minutes had stopped, and the physical weariness that had hung over me like a wet blanket had lifted. I knew the tests would come back clear, but I was still in awe when the doctors came into my room to give me the results of what was to be the last test before I was released to return home to die.

The doctor said, "We can't explain this, but, there is nothing wrong with you." It was a classic response from a medical professional encountering a supernatural healing without basis in science or medicine. Every trace of leukemia had miraculously vanished from my body! I left the hospital that day 100 percent healthy and knowing that God had healed me.

The Apostle Paul reminds us in 1 Corinthians 4:20 that the "kingdom of God is not a matter of talk but of power." My healing was undeniable evidence of the supernatural realm invading the natural. This was my first encounter with the supernatural. I not only experienced complete healing, but I knew beyond a shadow of a doubt that my grandfather had heard a personal message from God. Although it would be a few years until I surrendered my life to God, after that day in the hospital I was marked. At the time, I was very thankful to be healed by God, but I didn't understand what it meant to have a personal relationship with Him. I thought God had intervened in my life as a one-time event because of my grandfather's prayers. All I really knew was I had encountered the supernatural realm, and I was genuinely intrigued to know more.

After I gave my life to God in college, which I will tell you more about in chapter 2, my previous quest to explore science and the natural world became an insatiable search to encounter God and experience more of the supernatural.

Exploring the Supernatural

Scientists are devoting their lives to explore the depths of the natural realm, but who is giving their life to explore the depths of the supernatural? The current proposed budget for the US government to spend on scientific research and development is $143 billion a year.[5] That is just a fraction of what universities and businesses in the private sector spend researching science and the natural world. We often prioritize exploring the natural world, which is a very important search, but I think there is a much greater search waiting for us to begin, and we don't have to be scientists to participate.

The man whose name has become synonymous with science concurs. Albert Einstein once said, "I want to know how God created this world. I am not interested in this or that phenomenon, in the spectrum of this or that element. I want to know His thoughts; the rest are details."[6] Although Einstein never professed personal faith in God, he said God's thoughts are what he wanted to know more than anything else.

When I was younger, I wanted to be like Einstein because of the incredible advances he made in discovering aspects of the natural world, but now I want to be like Einstein because he realized all the scientific discoveries in the world pale in comparison to exploring the supernatural realm of knowing God's thoughts.

PART TWO

THE PRACTICAL SCIENCE OF HEARING FROM GOD

CHAPTER ONE

Questions

The best scientists and explorers have the attributes of kids! They ask questions and have a sense of wonder. They have curiosity. 'Who, what, where, why, when, and how!' They never stop asking questions, and I never stop asking questions, just like a five year old.

—SYLVIA EARLE, MARINE BIOLOGIST, EXPLORER, AUTHOR, AND LECTURER[1]

The art and science of asking questions is the source of all knowledge.

—THOMAS BERGER[2]

If any of you lacks wisdom, you should ask God, who gives generously to all without finding fault, and it will be given to you.

—JAMES 1:5

The first step in the scientific method is asking a question about something that is observed. The question can be a how, what, when, who, which, why, or where type question. It all boils down to what the scientist wants to learn. If the scientist wants to understand the cosmos better, he or she might ask, "How do sun flares affect the Earth?" or "What happens to space debris?"

Do you remember your early years in elementary school, when you planted a bean seed in a disposable cup? You probably didn't realize it at the time, but that was science, and you were being taught the first steps in the scientific method. The questions you might have asked include, "How do plants grow?" or "What happens to a seed when it is stuck deep in dark soil, moistened by water, and warmed by the sun?" As part of your experiment, your teacher probably presented some research on the topic, and you hypothesized that based on the effects of the soil, water, and sun your little bean seed would eventually sprout and become a bean plant.

The first step for making contact with God begins with a question(s) for Him. As a believer, I know that, as Creator and Lord of the universe, He has all wisdom and certainly has the answers to my questions. Questions similar to those listed above: "What is His will for me in my family, work, ministry, or career?" "Where does He want me to live?" "Which house should I purchase?" "Why is life so difficult during this season?" or "How should I discipline my child about his disobedience?"

As God, He desires to have a relationship with each of us where we have open communication: expressing our hearts and desires and questions to Him, and God expressing His heart and desires back to us, answering our questions with His wisdom and direction. I want that kind of relationship with God, and I'm sure you do, too. The question part is easy; everybody has questions for God. However, hearing the answers from God often seems to elude us. So, how does God answer our questions?

He Clears His Throat

I know I'm not the only one who has wished that God would speak with an audible voice or at least give an occasional message written in the sky when seeking Him for direction. Soon after giving my life to Jesus, I remember thinking many times, *God, I want to follow you and choose what you want me to choose. Why can't you just drop a blueprint from heaven? That would make this so much easier.*

God does not typically speak in an audible voice, and I have yet to receive a blueprint from heaven. However, I have found that He is true to His promise, as spoken through the prophet Jeremiah, "You will seek me and find me when you seek me with all your heart" (Jeremiah 29:13). It is important to note that God does not promise to be found by those who seek Him halfheartedly; but if our hearts are intent on seeking Him and obeying Him, we will find Him. The truth is, God wants to be found by those who really want to find Him.

I think about this truth when I play hide-and-go-seek with my boys. I can typically find where they are hiding in a matter of moments because I hear them giggling, wrestling around, or see their little feet hanging halfway out from under the bed. I think their favorite part of the game is when I find them. They hide in order to be found. I believe the same can be said of God. Meister Eckhart, a thirteenth-century German theologian, expressed this spiritual truth my boys taught me about the delight of being found: "God is like a person who clears His throat when hiding and so gives Himself away."[3]

The Old Testament prophet Isaiah said it like this: "Truly you are a God who has been hiding himself, the God and Savior of Israel" (Isaiah 45:15). Why does God remain hidden to a degree? Why does He not always speak to us in the overt ways we would so prefer? I believe He is looking for those who will look for Him because every true and sincere relationship is always a two-way relationship.

Proverbs 25:2 says, "It is the glory of God to conceal a matter; to search out a matter is the glory of kings." God loves it when we search Him out. He is inviting each one of us on a divine game of hide-and-go-seek, during which He clears His throat so that those who are listening can easily find Him. He wants to teach each of us how to discern His voice and promptings.

The longer you walk with Him and the more you value His voice in your life, the easier it is to discern. Hearing His voice has been compared to a radio picking up airwaves. Radio waves are constantly floating through the air, but you need a radio receiver to pick up the sounds. Like the radio waves, God is always speaking; we just have to learn to tune our frequency to hear what He is saying. Jesus explains in John 10:3–5 that hearing from God is meant to be a reality in every believer's life.

I know some churches teach that we can't hear His voice today. They teach that God only speaks through what is written in His Word: the Bible. God certainly speaks to us through His Word. The whole next chapter focuses on the ways that God speaks through the Bible and that nothing He speaks will ever contradict His written Word. However, the written Word is certainly not the only way He speaks.

Logos vs. Rhema

There are two Greek New Testament terms pastors often reference that are translated as "word" in the New Testament: *logos* and *rhema*. The first word, *logos*, refers to the written Word of God—the Bible—and also to the living Word, Jesus (see examples in Luke 8:11, John 1:1, Philippians 2:16). The second term, *rhema*, means an utterance or spoken word (found in Luke 1:38; 3:2; 5:5 and Acts 11:16).

For you and me, a *rhema* is the Holy Spirit speaking to us in the present moment, through thoughts, ideas, dreams, visions, and inner knowing or warning, and through the words of others: e.g., a preacher, counselor, friend, or even a total stranger. God's *rhema* word to us will usually deal with specific current circumstances and may give us direction, warning, or confirmation about something God wants us to do. However a *rhema* word will never contradict God's written Word—the Bible—the *logos*. In other words, God will never tell you to do something that is against principles in the Bible.

As you follow the steps outlined in this book, you will see that I encourage you, as you hear from God, to confirm what you believe God is saying to you by referring to the written Word (*logos*) and also share it with a trusted, spiritually mature friend. If God is really speaking to you, His words will stand up to the test and be confirmed by His written Word and His counsel through others.

Listening for the Voice

The one who enters by the gate is the Shepherd of the sheep. The gatekeeper opens the gate for him, and the sheep listen to his voice. He calls his own sheep by name and leads them out. When he has brought out all his own, he goes on ahead of them, and his sheep follow him because they know his voice. But they will never follow a stranger; in fact, they will run away from him because they do not recognize a stranger's voice. (John 10:2–5)

This passage teaches us that we have an active role to play in listening to His voice. In it, John explains that we follow Him because we know His voice and that we will not follow a stranger's voice.

I love how God speaks to us through metaphors so that we can understand spiritual truth through natural symbolism. One of the interesting facts I learned when I was studying about sheep for a weekend message is that they really do learn the voice of their particular shepherd. If there are a thousand sheep all together in a pasture and five hundred of the sheep belong to one shepherd, only five hundred sheep will respond to his call. The other five hundred will stay in the pasture because to them it is a stranger's voice calling and they have learned not to respond.

John 10:27 reiterates this same principle: "My sheep listen to my voice; I know them, and they follow me." Notice the passage does not say "my super-spiritual sheep" or "my full-time ministry sheep" will know my voice. It simply says my sheep will know my voice. This is a promise for all believers.

We learn to quickly recognize the voice of the ones we love and those whose voices have weight in our lives. I remember when my wife, Taryn, and I were dating in the days before cell phones and caller ID; I could recognize it was her voice as soon as the first word was out of her mouth. After thirteen years of marriage, her voice has become even more familiar to me. Let's say she calls and says, "Hey, babe!" and I say, "Who is this?" If she replies, "It's me," and I say, "Me who?" I don't have to be a prophet to know that I am going to be sleeping on the sofa that night.

Although I can't always recognize God's voice with the same clarity or certainty that I can recognize Taryn's, I have placed focus and effort into discerning and obeying His voice because I love Him and His words have weight in my life.

Discerning His Voice

How can we know we are hearing the voice of God versus the voice of the enemy or the voice of our personal desires? Ask yourself the following questions:

+ Is what I am hearing unclear or confusing?
+ Does what I hear contradict the Bible?
+ If I act on what I am hearing, will it lead me to compromise my values?

The voice of the enemy is often unclear and confusing, it frequently contradicts biblical truths, and it ultimately leads you into sin and compromise. In the Garden of Eden, the serpent deceived Eve by adding to, omitting, twisting, and questioning what God said. The confusion in his words contradicted the simple directions that God had given Adam and eventually led Adam and Eve into sin.

Satan did the same when he tempted Jesus in the wilderness. He quoted Scripture to Jesus, but the motive was to tempt Jesus toward selfishness so he would disobey the call of God. Satan pulled on the human desires that Jesus likely had for food and authority, but the offering was outside the will of God.

The key to discerning between God, the enemy, and our own voice comes by familiarity through practice. The longer you walk with God, the easier it becomes to distinguish between the three. It is often easiest to recognize the difference between God's voice and the enemy's voice; it is more difficult to distinguish between your human voice and God's.

It's okay if you can't readily discern God's voice at first. Don't let that uncertainty paralyze you. If what you're hearing seems like something that would be pleasing to God and agrees with His character and Word, take a step toward it as you remain in dialogue with the Lord, asking Him to redirect you if it is not the best path for you. God looks at the intention of the heart. If your heart's desire is to please Him, you can trust He will not let you miss anything.

Based on the three questions I asked above, if what you are hearing is unclear or confusing, wait until the direction is clear. If what you are hearing contradicts the Bible in any way, even if it seems clear, do not act on it. If what you are hearing will lead you into sin in your actions, attitude, or speech, it is not coming from God.

God is not a God of confusion, but of peace (see I Corinthians 14:33). God will never contradict His Word, and if He is speaking to you and leading you by His Spirit, He will never direct you into gratifying the desires of your flesh (see Galatians 5:16). Isaiah 30:21 says, "Whether you turn to the right or to the left, your ears will hear a voice behind you, saying, 'This is the way; walk in it.'" I have found that this voice brings joy, clarity, and further revelation, and even when I am not 100 percent sure of the origin of a thought, I can trust that as I continue to seek Him, He will guide me in the way I should walk, just as this verse promises.

There is a great story in 1 Kings Chapter 19. The great prophet Elijah had just come through a season of powerful ministry—he was physically, emotionally, and spiritually exhausted, and he was running in fear after being threatened by his enemy, Jezebel. In his exhaustion, Elijah's perspective becomes one of self-pity, but the Lord continues to minister to him, feeding him, providing water, and allowing him to sleep. God's desire is to restore his servant so he can continue with the call and purpose that God has for his life.

In verse 11, Elijah is hiding in a cave and God tells him to stand outside on the mountain because He is going to pass by. Then three dramatic signs happen. First, there is a wind that tore apart the mountain, but the Lord was not in the wind. Second, there was a great earthquake, but the

Lord was not in the earthquake. Third, there was a fire, but the Lord was not in the fire. After the fire there was a "still, small voice."

Although the wind, earthquake and fire were probably creation's dramatic response to the presence of the Lord, Elijah did not respond to any of these signs. It was when he heard the still, small voice of the Lord that the Bible says he put his cloak over his face and stood at the mouth of the cave to hear what God wanted to say. As Elijah responded to God's voice, he received his next set of directions.

As you learn to attune your ears to hear the voice of the Lord, there are a few things that can be produced or evidenced, so I encourage you to look for the following six occurrences:

1. **Strong Recurring Thought:** One of the most common ways I hear His voice is through a recurring thought or idea. As explained earlier, this is often a *rhema* word from God that comes through our thoughts. I have learned to pay close attention to my thoughts, especially recurring ones, and ask God if these are ideas from Him.

2. **An Idea with Genuine Excitement:** Generally when God is calling you to do something, there is an excitement about that area. But there are times when He calls you to do something difficult, so there is not a natural excitement about following through, but it is still typically superseded by the excitement of knowing that He is actively calling you and providing direction, and that He will be with you.

3. **Deep, Calming Peace:** Colossians 3:15 explains that God's peace will rule in our hearts—it is a gift He gives that helps guide us. His peace is a supernatural confirmation of His presence with us and a way He confirms where He is leading. We will explore this topic more thoroughly in chapter 4.

4. **An Inner Warning, Caution, or Check:** God in His kindness allows us to discern that certain decisions are not the wisest or best, or the direction may be right, but not the timing. It is up to us to heed these warnings and choose to go a different path or wait when we sense an inner check or caution.

5. **A Supernatural Knowing:** This is when you have a strong inclination about something that feels certain deep down, but that certainty is too deep to have a logical, natural understanding. This is more than intuition, as it is a supernatural understanding from the Lord. However, because of the subjective nature of our inclinations, we must test it, just as we test the other ways we hear from God.

6. **Open Doors:** Revelation 3:7 says that God will open doors that no man can shut and shut doors no man can open. We will explore this idea further in this chapter, but I encourage you to be looking for open doors of opportunity and to ask God if He is leading you through those doors. Obviously, not every door that opens before you is God leading you in that direction, but I have learned to look for open doors as a way that God leads and provides direction.

The Seeds of Vision

God subtly speaks to me every day through His still, small voice as well as little nudges and ideas that I know did not come from me or even through my desires. However, there have also been monumental times God has spoken to me that I would place in the game-changer category. I have documented each of these milestone moments in the back of my Bible with their corresponding date. One of the most significant game-changing moments came on April 22, 2005.

I was at a retreat center in the Shenandoah Valley for a doctoral course. Our professor, Dr. Mara Crabtree, taught the class about stewarding the dreams God had placed in our hearts. She shared a passage in Genesis explaining that there were many years between the time when Joseph first received the dream God had for his life and the time that the dream was fulfilled. She then gave us a handful of seeds that were supposed to represent the dreams God had placed in our hearts. Planting the seeds was meant to be symbolic of the season of stewarding our dreams before they came to fruition. With the rest of the class, I planted my seeds outside the chapel at the retreat center. I knew my seeds represented the church Taryn and I had long felt called by God to plant in the Washington, D.C., area.

Planting a church had been a dream in my heart since 1998, but the dream felt vague and seemed way too big for me. (This is actually a great litmus test to show that it is a God-sized dream. As Ephesians 3:20, says, He doesn't want to give us dreams we can accomplish with our own strengths or talents because He wants to show us that He can do immeasurably more through us than we could ask or even imagine.)

I had actually shared this dream with Taryn on our first date. Some guys may stick to the light stuff on the first date, like asking about the girl's favorite food or where she grew up, but evidently not me. I knew there was a call on both of our lives to do something great for God, and I began to pursue her to see if we were meant to walk together in the dream of planting a church in D.C. After I felt God's yes, I asked Taryn to marry me in the spring of 2002 (after a few obstacles and course corrections from God, which I will share in more detail in chapter 5). We were married that summer, and we both knew we were called to plant a life-giving, multicultural church in the Washington, D.C., area. What we didn't know was when or how it would happen.

After I planted the seeds my professor had given me, I looked down at the formation in which the seeds were planted—I noticed there were seventeen seeds planted in a circle and three above it to the side. At that moment, I sensed the Holy Spirit whisper, "You will plant seventeen churches in the D.C. metro area (the seventeen seeds represented the seventeen campuses we would plant around the D.C. area) and three up in New York (represented by the three seeds off to the side)." This was one of the clearest voices I have heard in my life, and I know that it was the Living God speaking to me. For the next two years Taryn and I continued to seek God and wait on His timing for how and when we should launch the church.

Look Expectantly

The Hebrew word for "wait" is *qavah*, meaning to "look expectantly." The definition demonstrates that waiting on the Lord is not a passive activity. Rather, it is actively seeking where He is moving, so we are ready to step forward when God says it's time.

Waiting on the Lord has been a significant theme in DC Metro Church's story. The spring before we launched in 2007, two of my closest friends from graduate school who would help me plant the church, Matt Stroia and Julie Reams, and I visited the D.C. area to fast, pray, and walk the streets asking God to reveal to us the location He had for what would become DC Metro Church. We investigated over twenty-five locations, knocked on countless doors, and even sent chocolates and flowers to one of the school superintendents, hoping the gesture would gain her favor and possibly an opportunity to use one of the area schools. All twenty-five-plus doors were closed—very humbling!

One day Matt was lying on his bed thinking about the future church when a Middle Eastern restaurant he had visited in Alexandria, Virginia, popped into his mind. He was puzzled as to why he was thinking about food. He was about to attribute it to random, wandering thoughts or hunger, when he decided to ask God if this thought was somehow connected to the church. He immediately thought about the movie theater, the Regal Potomac Yard Theater, down the street from the restaurant. Was this God's voice speaking through a picture in his mind's eye?

Thoughts and Ideas

Just as Matt experienced the thought of the Middle Eastern restaurant popping into his head, God will sometimes speak to us through thoughts, ideas, or a picture in our imaginations. In February 2014, I experienced God speaking to me through a **recurring thought.** DC Metro Church was close to making an offer on a large church facility in Maryland that was in foreclosure (the building was the size of one-and-a-half Walmart Supercenters). Our board had signed off on making an offer, and although I still didn't have complete peace about it, we were moving forward with an offer that we expected would be accepted.

A short time before the offer was to be made, I was sitting in a local pastors' gathering called City Fathers. Pastor Mark Batterson, who was leading the gathering, said he believed God was going to speak to each of us that day about our area of greatest need. As I bowed my head and was thinking about that potential property, a thought came to my mind: *Take Virginia first!* It was a thought that I heard over and over again that day at the gathering and many times over the following weeks. For me and the church, it was God's direction that we not purchase the property in Maryland but focus future expansion in Virginia—something that is happening as I write.

Another time I experienced Him speaking to me through a **great idea.** I was on my way home to spend a date night with my wife. The church was in the middle of a fast from food and media, so I couldn't take her to a restaurant or to a movie. I wanted to have a special date night with my wife and asked the Lord if He had any ideas of what we could do together. I had a thought that was too good to be mine: take Taryn to all the houses God had provided for us to live in during our time in D.C., and other places significant to what He had done through DC Metro Church. As we stopped in front of each location, we took time to pray a prayer of thanks for God's blessings. The God-inspired idea was both spiritual and romantic!

God can speak to us through thoughts, ideas, and through pictures in our imaginations in which, instead of hearing words or thoughts, we see an image. Similar to the other ways that God speaks to us, you should validate these thoughts, ideas, and images to what is in the written Word (the Bible) and, when necessary, submit to godly counsel. The source of our thoughts can be God, self, or even the enemy, so it is important to test them. Remember, nothing from God will contradict the Bible. If you are unclear of the source or interpretation of a thought, it can be tested and weighed with the help of some spiritually mature friends.

The absolutely incredible part of the story is that while Matt was having this interaction with God, God was also speaking to me about the movie theater. I had just heard about a church in Florida that had started in a movie theater, so I began to research theaters in the Alexandria area. I had the Regal movie theater website still open on my computer when Matt called me that afternoon to ask me my thoughts on starting the church in the Potomac Yard Theater. Talk about an incredible confirmation that this was the location we were to pursue! Needless to say, I immediately contacted the theater to see if they would be open to a church meeting in one of the theaters. After a ton of discouraging closed doors, this door essentially flew open . . . and the rest, as they say, is history. The moment we secured the theater, I was overwhelmingly thankful for all the closed doors, knowing that all twenty-five-plus facilities that rejected us paled in comparison to the theater.

We had a similar journey while searching for our first campus location. Because the Lord had so clearly spoken to me in 2005 that the church would have seventeen campuses throughout the D.C. area and three in the New York area, becoming a multisite church had been in our hearts from the beginning. What the Lord did not tell me was when or how. During the third year of the church, we began seeking God to see if it was time to start the first campus. Over the next two years we went to go see more than thirty potential campus locations. Similar to our search five years earlier, we encountered closed door after closed door . . . until—you guessed it—we approached another Regal movie theater, this time in Fairfax, Virginia.

Throughout the process, we had been praying the prayer from Revelation 3:7 that says, "These are the words of him who is holy and true, who holds the key of David. What he opens no one can shut, and what he shuts no one can open." The Fairfax area was already on the radar of our leadership team as a strategic area to start our first campus, so we were thrilled when this location opened up. We saw God's fingerprints in this choice, as our first sanctuary was a Regal movie theater in Potomac Yard. Somehow it seemed right in step that the door God chose to open for our first campus would bring us back to our roots in a Regal theater. Thus, we officially became one church in two locations on January 13, 2013, as we launched our Fairfax campus.

When God Says No!

The number of closed doors we experienced before we initially launched the church and the first campus illustrates an important principle we find in the Apostle Paul's life in Acts 16. God often speaks through a no before He says yes to what is actually the very best choice for us. I am not always the biggest fan of hearing God say no because I am so ready for Him to say yes, but I have seen time and time again how the no is actually a gift, as He is at work to bring into alignment His best and highest for me.

Modern day amateur theologian Garth Brooks had this same revelation in his song "Unanswered Prayer," which hit number one on the Country Billboards in the 1990s. Brooks talks about taking his wife to a hometown football game and running into his girlfriend from high school. As he introduces the two women, he begins to remember how much he had desired his girlfriend back in the day, praying each night that if God would give her to him for all time, he would never ask for anything again.

Although he doesn't tell us what had happened to the old girlfriend over the years, Brooks ends the song thanking God for unanswered prayers, reminding us that God still cares even if He doesn't answer prayers the way we want Him to—and that some of His greatest gifts are those unwanted answers. God always answers, but sometimes His answer is "in a different way" or "in a different time" because He sees from a perspective we cannot and He can be trusted to work all things together for good, even when it is not what we would have chosen at the time. I think all of us in hindsight can thank God for His no's to some of the prayers in our lives. As author Tim Keller says, "God will either give us what we ask or give us what we would have asked if we knew everything he knows."[4]

We see this same principle of God saying no before He says yes to direct the Apostle Paul where to go in Acts 16. When teaching others to hear God's voice, I often choose the Apostle Paul as my biblical example because he did not walk with Jesus while Jesus was on the earth. The other apostles had the advantage of hearing His voice before His ascension, but Paul had his first encounter with the ascended Jesus on the road to Damascus in Acts 9. Like you and me, he had to learn to discern the promptings and leadings of the Holy Spirit. From the start of Paul's ministry in Acts 9 until Acts 16, we see that he received very distinct direction on where to go and what to do, but it does not clearly explain how he determined where to go until Acts 16. In fact, I believe Acts 16 reveals his grid for how you and I can discern His voice.

In Acts 16:6–10, there is a process that Paul is taken through that gives much insight on how to discern the guidance of the Holy Spirit for our own lives.

> They passed through the Phrygian and Galatian region, having
> been forbidden by the Holy Spirit to speak the word in Asia; and
> after they came to Mysia they were trying to go into Bithynia and
> the Spirit of Jesus did not permit them; and passing by Mysia,

they came down to Troas. A vision appeared to Paul in the night, a man of Macedonia was standing and appealing to him and saying, "Come over to Macedonia and help us." When he had seen the vision, immediately we sought to go into Macedonia concluding that God had called us to preach the gospel to them.

In Acts 16:6 we see Paul learning where he is not to go. It seems to reveal that if there is a place that we specifically should not go, then we can infer that there is a place that we are to go. It is significant to observe that the passage says the Spirit of Jesus would not let them go. I don't know about you, but I had to learn the hard way that it is not worth it to push ahead if God does not want me to go somewhere. Now when I feel a hesitation in my spirit or a check from the Lord about a certain direction, I have learned to more quickly say, "I'm not going."

The next thing we observe from the text is that Paul comes to the end of the road in Troas. It seems highly probable that Paul came to a point here where he started to doubt. He had just tried to go two other places, and they were both obviously blocked by the hand of God—let's call them closed doors. Perhaps he thought God was going to block everywhere and anywhere he wanted to go, or perhaps he wondered if he was listening more closely to his own voice rather than God's.

This is helpful to remember when we are having trouble discerning the will of God. Even Paul, the man God used to change the course of history in the Roman world, could not always immediately know God's direction. I've learned that to enjoy this process with God, I have to focus on the outcome or reward rather than on any delays or setbacks. It's similar to eating a Cadbury Creme Egg. You have to unwrap it and break through the chocolate "shell" in order to get to the center—a tasty surprise better than you could even imagine. God delights in the relationship and trust that is formed when we have to continue to look to and depend on Him for each step of the journey.

I like to call this "progressive revelation" where He gives us just what we need to know exactly when we need to know it. I naturally prefer to know where the path is going to lead before I start my journey, but God kindly reminds me that He is walking with me and that it's His path, not mine. He invites me to enjoy the adventures we will go on together and promises to help me navigate every twist and turn along the way—and at the end of the day that is all I need to know.

In verse 9, we see that in the night, in what may have been Paul's moment of despair, a vision came to him. All Scripture tells us is that it came to him "in the night." It is not stated whether he was sleeping and he woke up or if the vision came to him as he walked along the road. However, the most important thing is the content of his vision—it was of a man that needed his help in Macedonia.

Dreams and Visions

Two additional ways God will speak to us is through dreams and visions. There is a prophetic word that appears in the Old Testament book of Joel and later in Acts 2:17. The word talks about God pouring out His Spirit on all mankind in the last days. One of the results of this outpouring will be that "Your old men will dream dreams, your young men will see visions" (Joel 2:28). The difference between a dream and a vision is that a dream takes place while you are asleep and a vision occurs while you are awake.

In a dream, God's Spirit often speaks to you through images. Sometimes the meaning of a God-inspired dream is very clear—a warning, a blessing, or a sense of direction for something you had asked God about earlier. Other times the meaning is not so clear and will need some interpretation.

As a disclaimer, not all dreams are God inspired. Our dreams can be influenced by different stimuli: random people and events strung together through subconscious thoughts, a mind that is racing with thoughts from your busy day, or even from the enemy. When in doubt if a dream is from God, or when you don't understand the meaning of a dream you believe is from Him, ask Him for the wisdom to understand. James 1:5 affirms that God wants to give us wisdom if we ask.

A vision is like a spiritual movie playing in front of us or in our heads while we are awake and conscious. Like a dream, the vision may be clear in meaning, or it may need some additional interpretation and understanding from God. If you do experience dreams or visions, submit them to the process we are introducing in this book. See if the dream or vision's message is supported by the Bible (God will never contradict His written Word) and submit it to someone who is spiritually mature and whose counsel you trust.

Paul's night vision reveals something about the way God guides, but it also reveals something about Paul's heart. Paul was partnered with God. It seems to reveal that he sincerely wanted to go where he could help people. Why else would the Lord give him a vision of someone needing help? The Lord did this because He knew that Paul wanted to go where he would be used to help people. Here we see God's sovereignty in choosing to guide Paul in a way that would relate to desires in his heart. Once we submit our hearts and lives to Christ and begin growing closer to Him, God often uses the desires of our heart to guide us into His will. Psalm 37:4 says, "Take delight in the Lord, and He will give you the desires in your heart," but we must remember to look at Psalm 37:4–5, which says, "Commit everything you do to the Lord, trust in Him, and He will do this." These verses are a great reminder that although the Lord directs us through our desires when we are surrendered to Him, our role is to commit everything to Him, trust Him, and receive His help, just as we see modeled in Paul's life in Acts 16.

In verse 9, the Greek word *parakaleo* is translated into the English as "appealing to him" in reference to the man from Macedonia. This word means, "To call to, to beseech, and to exhort."[5] This brings us to a greater depth of understanding on what the passage is really stating. Further insight is gained by noting that the use of this word is "to call someone to oneself," not "to call to someone." It is evident from the Greek word chosen that this man in Macedonia needed help and that it did not matter where the help came from; it just mattered that the help came to him.

It is also significant to note that once Paul received guidance from the Lord, he was confident in putting that guidance into motion immediately. This word is derived from the Greek word *eutheos*, which means, "suddenly and straightway."[6] Thoralf Gilbrant explains in *The New Testament Greek-English Dictionary*, "Paul and his company did not hesitate once this positive guidance was given. They concluded that God had called them, therefore they acted."[7] It is said that slow obedience is no obedience. Paul's expedient obedience should be a model to all believers, that when we do receive guidance from the Lord, we are to act upon it quickly.

As we take a closer look, we can begin to see a pattern of guidance that the Lord used in Paul's life, especially concerning the geographic location of ministry. It is interesting to note that Paul's discernment came in two steps. First, God told Paul where not to go. Only after Paul was obedient to those instructions, God told him where he was to go. This is not always the pattern, but as we discussed earlier, one of the ways in which God often speaks is that He closes wrong doors before He opens the right one.

God wants the type of relationship with us where we speak to Him and He speaks to us. His speaking to us can happen in many different ways: through His written Word—the Bible, a rhema word, thoughts and ideas, pictures and images, dreams and visions, an inner knowing, or even through closed or open doors. As you experience God in Step One of the 40-Day Challenge, get ready to submit your questions to Him. You will then have the opportunity to record the preliminary answers you think you have received in Step Two of the process: The Research.

CHAPTER TWO

Research

"Research is to see what everybody else has seen, and to think what nobody else has thought."

—ALBERT SZENT-GYORGYI, HUNGARIAN BIOCHEMIST[1]

"Somewhere, something incredible is waiting to be known."

—DR. CARL SAGAN, AMERICAN ASTRONOMER, WRITER, AND SCIENTIST[2]

"Study to shew thyself approved unto God, a workman that needeth not to be ashamed, rightly dividing the word of truth."

—2 TIMOTHY 2:15 KJV[3]

The second step in the scientific method is research. For the scientist, this means using all the available tools—scientific journals, the internet, other scientists—to gain the most information about how to answer the question being researched. Researching and collecting as much information as possible before starting to experiment helps the scientist create his or her plan for answering the question and for making sure mistakes from the past aren't repeated.

Likewise, in this book the second step to hearing from God consists of research that helps to either answer the question we just asked in Step One, or to confirm the answer we think we've already received from God. As I've mentioned, I have asked God to speak to me in dramatic ways, and I love it when He does. However, I have found I often seek a spectacular outward sign from Him instead of spending my time in Scripture— in research, "rightly dividing the word of truth" (2 Timothy 2:15 NKJV)[4] and asking Him to speak to me through His Word.

He Speaks through His Word

God loves to reveal Himself to those who are seeking Him—digging deeper—through His Word. Jeremiah 29:13 says, "You will seek me and find me when you seek me with all your heart." In applying this verse, I have found that the more I seek Him in His Word, the more He will speak.

When I was growing up, I had a distant respect for God's Word, but I also thought reading it was extremely boring and best suited for those in the retirement community. I viewed the Bible as a book with antiquated stories and as a manual on how to be good. Being good seemed quite dull, and I felt a certain cognitive dissonance (believing in the truth of Scripture but also feeling a distancing ennui) whenever I heard someone read from the Bible. I went to church every Sunday, but I definitely did not love His Word.

In my high school and college years I drifted further from Jesus. During my junior year in college, I decided to spend a semester in Utah, away from all my LSU fraternity brothers, in an attempt to get a fresh start. After a semester of searching for the meaning of life to no avail, taking a myriad of drugs, and essentially living my same hedonistic lifestyle, I reached a low point. My move was an attempt to escape, but change seemed elusive. I could not escape myself.

However, while waiting for my parents at the airport when they were coming to visit me, a man handed me a little book—an orange Gideons Bible containing the New Testament, Psalms, and Proverbs. My first thought was to tuck it away in my junk drawer, but my curiosity got the best of me. I opened to the book of Proverbs, and I could not put it down. Little did I know that the content in that little orange book would change the trajectory of my life. The wisdom and insight found in the verses of Proverbs seemed to leap off the page. How could this be the same book I had written off as obsolete and irrelevant years before?

This began my journey into reading through the New Testament and surrendering my life to this man named Jesus who fascinated me. Over the years I can honestly say that I have fallen in love with the Bible. The more I love God's Word and revere it, digging into it, researching the truth between its covers, and meditating on its meaning, the more I recognize Him speaking to me. The same can happen for you, too. God wants all believers to truly love His Word and to hear Him speak with specific and personal clarity.

It's Alive!

One of my favorite passages in the Bible is Hebrews 4:12 because it reminds us that God desires to speak to us and shape us through His Word: "For the Word of God is *alive* and active (emphasis mine). Sharper than any double-edged sword, it penetrates even to dividing soul and spirit, joints and marrow; it judges the thoughts and attitudes of the heart." Do you know of any other book that claims to be alive?

The Holy Spirit causes God's Word to come alive so that we are pierced, or penetrated, to the core and empowered supernaturally to apply what we read to our lives. The Bible was written to be an invitation into an interactive conversation with God rather than just another book containing some stories, wise sayings, and principles. This means that although I can read the same passage again and again, the Holy Spirit will highlight new aspects each time or teach me how the passage applies to a particular circumstance. I love how specific and personal the Lord is and never tire of it.

For example, I was reading through Psalm 78 one morning before we moved my family across town into a new home. Taryn and I were already a little nervous for the kids and us, as it was a bit outside of town—we were moving to "the country." While reading Psalm 78, I felt the Holy Spirit highlight verse 55, "He drove out nations before them and allotted their lands to them as an inheritance; he settled the tribes of Israel in their homes." A wave of peace came over me as I felt God speak a promise to me through His Word, *David, just as I settled the Israelites in their home, so I will settle you, Taryn, and your boys in your home.*

That Word from the Lord came at the perfect time. I have found that no matter how much we plan and prepare, moving is an unsettling ordeal. What encouraged me most was that I felt like He was saying that He would turn our house into a home—that He would truly settle us. I wrote "January 2012—Psalm 78:55" in the back of my Bible. I wanted to remember this promise from God and claim it as we transitioned. I can say now, this Word truly came to pass as we made the move. The boys love our new place because of all the surrounding woods for them to explore, and it has become a respite to create memories together as a family. We feel truly settled.

Not long after our move, I was reading in Jeremiah 30 and verse 2 stood out to me: "This is what the Lord, the God of Israel, says: 'Write in a book all the words I have spoken to you.'" I've always dreamed of writing a book, but I needed some momentum and direction from God as to when to start. As I read this verse, I felt God giving me the green light to begin writing. From this, I also realized His hand would be upon it as I recorded the words He had spoken to me. I wrote "April 2012—Jeremiah 30:2–3" in the back of my Bible because it was my word from the Lord to begin the book you are reading now.

Confirmation Through the Word

On the morning of June 15, 2010, I saw a vision—an animated picture in my mind's eye—during my time with God. In the vision I was standing on the bridge that is adjacent to our current church facility and looking at our new building. I saw not only our current building but another large facility next door, as plain as day. Next, I saw myself in the facility in what I understood to be a several-stories-high prayer tower overlooking Washington, D.C., and the monuments. I was surrounded by my four kids, who looked like they were teenagers, and they were praying with me for the city of D.C. I began to scribble the vision of what I saw on a nearby napkin. I sensed in my spirit that God was calling us to take steps toward acquiring the building and land next door to our facility, but I was not sure when or how it would happen.

We had just gone through an arduous year-and-a-half process of acquiring permits and renovating our current facility to be able to move in just two months prior. It was a significant step in faith because our budget had to double to pay the bills in the new facility. I heard the still, small voice of God telling us to acquire that first facility, confirmed it with DC Metro Church's Lead Team and Overseers, and stepped out in faith. (In chapter 3 we will talk about the importance of seeking counsel when you are making important decisions.) God was completely true to His Word. In one month the budget of DC Metro doubled, which had not happened before and has not happened since. After that season of being stretched in the area of faith, the last thing on my mind was trying to acquire more property. I thought it might be time to have a relaxing, low-key summer, but evidently God had other plans.

During that time, I was studying the book of Joshua. The theme of the passages I was reading was about the Israelites possessing the Promised Land. As I read, I felt Him stirring my heart about the call that He has on DC Metro not only to possess physical land, but to partner with Him in repossessing the land spiritually. There is a rich spiritual heritage upon which our country was founded, a godly foundation that our forefathers sought to implement. Unfortunately, we have veered away from that foundation, but God, in His mercy, is calling us to help restore a God-first culture throughout the D.C. metro area.

In Joshua 6, Joshua leads the Israelites to march and pray around the city of Jericho as a prophetic declaration of the land they would possess. After reading this and praying about the vision God had given me of the property next door, I felt led to go do my own Jericho march around the property. But there was one significant obstacle: a gate around the property and a security guard in front of the building. I figured that if the Israelites could go boldly into Jericho to possess the Promised Land that was filled with their enemies, then I could take down the security guard. (I am only kidding!)

As a pastor, I decided it might be wise to try a different approach. I convinced Dana Sorensen, a staff member who has been a part of the church since the beginning, to go with me to try and convince the security guard to let us walk around the building. I was sure the guard was going to think we were crazy and was ready for her to turn us down, when she said (to my surprise), "Sure, you can walk around the building, as long as I walk with you." The three of us began to circumnavigate the building. Pamela, the security guard, began to tell us her story. It happened to be her first night on the job, and she shared how she was a believer who had recently returned to the Lord. When we were halfway around the building she blurted out, "This may sound strange to you, but I feel like Rahab in the Bible who allowed Joshua and Caleb to spy out the land." Dana and I couldn't believe our ears. Did she just compare us to Joshua and Caleb? She had no idea that I had been studying the book of Joshua or that God had just given me a vision about possessing the land.

I believed in divine appointments before that night, but this further confirmed my belief that God absolutely is in the details of our life and that He strategically places certain people in our lives for a specific purpose. As if that were not enough, God in His kindness wanted to bring me further confirmation. Two nights later, on June 19, we had the incredible privilege of Christine Caine coming to speak at our church. Chris Caine is one of the most passionate, dynamic preachers I know, as she has acquired a reputation for speaking prophetic word through the message she brings to each particular church. I felt especially excited about what Chris would preach that night. Believe it or not, her message was the story of Joshua and Caleb spying out the land from the same passage in Joshua I had been studying. At one point in the message, she pointed in the direction of the property next door and loudly proclaimed, "God is calling you to possess the land!" Dana and I were having trouble containing ourselves as we looked at each other with wide eyes and knowing smiles. God was confirming through His Word what He had shown me earlier in a vision.

Holy Txt Challenge

A few years after we planted DC Metro Church, God spoke to me to help the church learn what it means to fall in love with the Bible. In a still, small voice I heard the instruction *Read my Word.* I realized that God was leading me to read His Word aloud to the church to awaken their hearts to Scripture in a greater way. "Read my Word" was the game changer that inspired what I aptly called the Holy Txt Challenge.

The challenge was, if one thousand people committed to reading their Bibles for twenty minutes a day for forty days, I would read the entire New Testament straight through, out loud, in one consecutive reading. They unabashedly rose to the challenge. On Friday, May 11, 2012, at 7 p.m., the marathon began—I sat in the front of the sanctuary and began reading from Matthew. I had excitement in my heart and expectancy in my spirit because I know that something significant happens as we declare His powerful Word aloud.

The most exhilarating part of the challenge was reading the last book—Revelation. The sanctuary was filled with a tangible faith and a palpable electricity, as so many members joined us for the reading of the final book of the New Testament. On Saturday, May 12, a little after 5 p.m., I completed approximately twenty-two hours of reading 260 chapters, 7,956 verses, and 138,020 words (and I consumed twenty cups of tea, twenty-four bottles of water, and three-and-a-half bears of honey). My part of the Holy Txt Challenge was finished, but the catalytic effects were just beginning.

One member shared, "During the Holy Txt Challenge, I felt the Word of God come alive for me like never before. My goodness! It was like all the cogs to an engine were coming into place in my head and heart as different pieces of the New Testament were being read, and then that engine started to turn, and revelation after revelation starting forming and gaining traction."

Another member explained, "After hearing the reading of the whole New Testament, the Word became so much more approachable for me. I never realized that the whole book of Matthew could be read in approximately two hours. The Holy Txt Challenge created a desire for me to read and study the Bible more on my own, so that I can unlock its treasures."

Reflecting back to when God told me that He wanted the people of our church to fall even more in love with His Word, I am encouraged to see how their desire to read and know its promises has increased. I am convinced that your love for it will grow, too, as you are faithful to read, study, and obey what it says. As A. W. Tozer said, "The Bible is not an end in itself, but a means to bring men to an intimate and satisfying knowledge of God, that they may enter into Him and delight in His Presence . . ."[5]

S-O-A-P

Oftentimes people ask me how I study the Bible. They want to know what research methods I use as I seek to answer my questions. My devotional times are very simple. I begin with a formula I learned years ago called S-O-A-P, created by Wayne Cordeiro. S-O-A-P stands for Scripture, Observation, Application, and Prayer.[6]

Scripture

The first step is simply to decide which passage you are going to study and then begin reading it. In the 40-Day Challenge at the back of the book, I've provided one scripture passage for each day. After completing the forty days, I recommend choosing a book of the Bible that you want to read, or doing a topical study with the help of a concordance. Some good books in the Bible to start with are the Gospel of John, any of Paul's letters in the New Testament, such as Ephesians or Philippians, or Psalms in the Old

Testament. Proverbs is great as well, as it has thirty-one chapters, providing a solid chapter a day for a month.

If you are interested in reading narratives about the lives of great men and women, I recommend tracing the story of the patriarchs in Genesis, Moses and the Israelites' escape from Egypt in the book of Exodus, the adventures of King David in 1 and 2 Samuel, or Peter and Paul in the book of Acts.

If you prefer a topical study, you can use a concordance to find what you are interested in and follow the passages and verses provided about that topic. Many study Bibles have concordances in the back, or you can find incredible concordances online at locations such as biblestudytools .com. Another good website is BibleGateway.com. There you can type the keyword you want to learn more about, and it will list all of the places that word appears in the Bible.

For example, if I am studying about purpose, I would look up the word *purpose*, and it would lead me to verses such as Psalm 138:7–8a, "Though I walk in the midst of trouble, you preserve my life; you stretch out your hand against the anger of my foes, with your right hand you save me [NIV]. The Lord will fulfill [His purpose] for me, [ESV]" or Proverbs 19:21, "Many are the plans in a person's heart, but it is the Lord's purpose that prevails." I recommend choosing a chapter, if you are studying a book, or a few verses if you are doing a topical study. Once you have your chapter or verses selected, you are ready to move to the O, or observation stage.

Observation

As you read Scripture, ask yourself, *What stands out?* Ask God, *What are you highlighting to me today?* For example, when I was studying the book of Joshua, the verse found in Joshua 1:8 stood out to me, "Keep this Book of the Law always on your lips; meditate on it day and night, so that you may be careful to do everything written in it. Then you will be prosperous and successful."

Here are some questions you can ask in the observation stage:

+ What is the historical/contextual situation?

+ When was it written?

+ To whom is it speaking?

+ Why was it written?

+ What kind of literary genre is it (narrative, command, poetry, or prophecy)?

+ How does the author arrange the text? Look for repeated words or phrases and theological words. (You can look these up if you do not know a definition or want to explore further.)

+ What does the passage say about God, Jesus, and the Holy Spirit?

+ What does the passage say about the believer?

+ What is the theme of the passage (the big idea)?

+ What are the main principles you learn from this text (timeless truths)?

+ What does the commentary or study Bible say about this passage, and how does that add to your understanding?

A few observations I wrote about Joshua 1:8:

1. This passage is a command to "Keep this book of the law always."

2. There are three things we are commanded to do with the book of the law: speak about it ("on your lips"); continually think about it ("meditate on it day and night"); and, act on it ("do everything written in it").

3. The result of us fulfilling this command is biblical prosperity and success.

After you finish writing down some observations, you can move to the A, or the Application step, where you try to determine how the passage applies to your personal life.

Application

For the Application step, I made up my own acronym, GOD SPA, which helps me ask intentional questions in order to apply the passage to my life. Besides, who doesn't like a little spa action? I want not only to read the Word, I also want to let it read me. When you let the Word read you, you are allowing God to speak to you through His Word so that you can apply its teachings to your life rather than just reading the words for cognitive knowledge. James 1:23–24 says: "Anyone who listens to the word but does not do what it says is like someone who looks at his face in a mirror and, after looking at himself, goes away and immediately forgets what he looks like."

Here are the six questions for you to ask to help you apply James 1:23–24:

1. G (Growth)—Is there an area where God is calling you to grow?

Is there a part of God's Word that you know you are not walking in the fullness of what God has for you? Perhaps God is revealing something in your heart. Maybe He is highlighting a relationship or an area in your marriage that needs work. Perhaps it is in your finances, your health, or something going on at work. Whichever area you feel Him revealing, I encourage you to surrender it to Him and ask Him to help you give Him full leadership.

2. O (Obedience)—Is there an area where God is calling you to obey?

Is there an area in your life that you are not obeying God right now? This can be similar and even overlapping with a growth area, but it is generally focused either on a specific action that you feel the Holy Spirit is asking you to take or a particular command in His Word that you know you have not been following.

As I often tell my boys, delayed obedience is not really obedience. Like any good parent, God wants our wholehearted obedience, so we should honestly be asking the Holy Spirit if there is any area where we are not walking in full obedience. God will graciously meet us in that place to give us His strength to help us turn from these areas, as we are honest and authentic before Him.

3. D (Direction)—Is there a direction God is speaking to you through this passage?

We all desire God's perspective on what we should do next in life. One of my favorite verses on direction is Psalm 32:8, which says, "I will instruct you and teach you in the way you should go." I have found one of the most common ways that God gives me direction is through my time in the Bible. When I have a decision coming up, I will allow myself some private time to pray and read, giving myself the space and quiet to see if God highlights anything through Scripture. I find that, time and again, He leads me to just the right passage, whether it be through my daily reading, a verse someone shares with me, or through one of my topical studies I explained earlier. God loves to guide us through His Word.

4. S (Sin)—Is there a sin God wants you to confess and turn from in this passage?

Sin sometimes sounds like a really religious word, but the Greek definition of sin is actually an archery term that means to "miss the mark." Often when I am reading the Word, God will bring to mind a certain area of my life, and I will realize that I haven't hit the mark in that area.

If God points out an area in your life where you have missed the mark, you need to do two things: repent and confess. The Greek word for repentance, *metanoia*, means changing your mind about a former attitude or action. You repent by recognizing that that attitude or action was wrong toward God or other people and choosing to change your mind and turn away from it. Confession is a part of repentance. It is telling God you are sorry for missing the mark. And not just saying the words, but really meaning them in your heart. The beauty is that 1 John 1:9 tells us that "If we confess our sins, he is faithful and just and will forgive us our sins and purify us from all unrighteousness."

Conviction vs. Condemnation

I have found it extremely helpful to know the difference between conviction and condemnation. Conviction is when God points out sin in your life because He wants you to know that He has something better for you and that He will help empower you to choose His path. It is often an action that God wants you to take such as, "Apologize to your co-worker for being selfish when you took the last sandwich at the luncheon without checking to see if he had eaten."

Condemnation is altogether different and from a different source. Condemnation is an attack from the enemy on your identity where he makes you feel guilty and weighed down. It is typically an accusation about who he says you are instead of a particular action you have done. For example, "You are a selfish person who is always looking out for yourself at the expense of others, and you'll never change."

As believers, we need to know how to discern between conviction and condemnation. Conviction is life-giving and empowering. It is never easy to face up to the mistakes in our lives, but when God highlights an area where we have missed the mark, He does it because He loves us and will give us the power to change as we surrender it to Him. Simply put, condemnation attacks your identity or character and often leaves you feeling hopeless and shameful while conviction guides you back to God's highest path for you and seeks to empower you for change.

5. P (Promise)—Is there a promise from this passage you can claim for your life?

Did you know that there are over six thousand promises in God's Word? For example, the passage Joshua 1:8 that we discussed earlier contains a clear promise: God promises that as I meditate and walk in the truths of His Word, He will make my way prosperous and successful. This is an example of a conditional promise, meaning God will fulfill His part on the condition that you fulfill your part.

We all would like to have what I call "God success" in our lives. In fact, the Hebrew translation of the word *prosper* means "to be pushed forward in life." How exciting is it to know that if we commit to read God's Word, He will push us forward in life? God's Word is filled with promises that we can cling to and pray over ourselves when we are in a hard situation or when we need to be reminded of His truth.

6. A (Accountability)—Is there any area where you need accountability?

Accountability is a key to success, because whenever you come across one of the five application areas in your Bible study, there is probably an area where you're thinking to yourself, *You know what? I don't know if I'm going to be able to walk this out on my own. I know I've got God's help, but I think it would be wise to call someone to hold me accountable in this area.*

Many times, after spending time in the Word, I've picked up the phone to call one of my accountability partners. I have three men whom I can call and say, "God is dealing with me, and I need you to regularly ask me about this area of my life."

By the way, no one can hold you accountable unless you tell that person where you're tempted or struggling. If they don't know your weakness, they're just going to ask you a general question, such as "Hey, how are you doing?" and we are most likely to answer, "Fine." I'm fine because I don't want to talk to you about my real issues. Did you know that when we avoid accountability, what we're actually saying is we don't really want to change? Because it is so important to be transparent in your accountability, having safe friendships where there is mutual trust is paramount. In chapter 3, I will share with you how to find and develop these types of relationships.

I ask all six of these GOD SPA questions for each passage I study. Typically, God will lead me to focus on a couple of these areas to highlight how He wants me to apply its message.

For example, from Joshua 1:8, I felt led to focus on Growth, Promise, and Accountability. I was challenged to increase my time in meditating on the Word (Growth) so that I can experience true success (Promise). I shared this challenge I was sensing with a few close friends who hold me accountable. After some dialogue with them and processing how I could implement this, I felt encouraged and empowered to increase my time of intentionally studying and meditating on God's Word.

Prayer

Using our S-O-A-P acrostic, we've discussed Scripture, Observation, and Application. The final P in S-O-A-P is Prayer. Prayer is actually the most important step and one of the most overlooked. This is simply taking whatever God has spoken to you and bringing it back to Him, asking Him to help you. You might pray, "God I'm going to need some help with this. I'm going to try to walk this out today."

A great support for this step is two-way prayer journaling: writing down your thoughts to God and then writing what you believe God is speaking to you. King David was one of the toughest, fiercest warriors in Scripture, and he was a voracious journal-er. A good portion of the book of Psalms is essentially David's journals crying out to the Lord and then listening and responding to what he hears. David received the plans for rebuilding the temple during one of his times of journaling. "'All this,' David said [in 1 Chronicles 28:19], 'I have in writing as a result of the Lord's hand on me, and he enabled me to understand all the details of the plan.'"

The prophet Habakkuk was no stranger to journaling. The first chapter of Habakkuk is essentially Habakkuk complaining to the Lord—which is a good reminder that we can be totally authentic with God when we are praying. Habakkuk asks God why it is taking Him so long to move regarding Habakkuk's situation. Before God answers, He instructs Habakkuk to write down his answer. Habakkuk 2:2 says, "Write down this vision; clearly inscribe it on tablets so one may easily read it" (HCSB).

In my first decade of walking with God, I definitely did not love journaling. I watched Taryn pour her heart out in journal after journal during the years we were dating and the first years of marriage, but I just couldn't get into it. Several years ago, at a retreat, my seminary professor challenged us to journal to God and then write what we were sensing He was saying to us. I had previously thought of journaling as just writing to myself, so writing to God felt a little strange, but when I realized I could write prayers to God and then listen for His reply, it became an entirely new experience for me.

I now love journaling and average about eight journals a year. As I have coached others in journaling, the method I teach is to write a letter to God and then write a letter back from God. I have heard countless others say that this brought a breakthrough in hearing from Him. One lady recently shared that as she practiced this technique of writing to herself from God, she was getting so many responses in her mind that she had trouble writing fast enough.

I am confident that God wants to bring a breakthrough in your walk with Him, too, and I encourage you to give it a try. To break it down, I first write God a letter where I am very honest and authentic before Him. I might include what I read in Scripture that day and if there were any challenges, revelations, or insights I want to remember. I thank Him for who He is and how good He is to me. I try to release any burdens I am still carrying and invite Him to speak into any of the problems or situations that are concerning me. I typically ask the Lord some questions about direction I am seeking or whatever is on my mind that day. I lift up my family, the church, and the people who are in my heart, asking Him to move in their lives and allowing space for Him to speak to me about any messages I should be conveying to others.

Next comes the fun part, where you write a letter to yourself from God. The first time I did this, I will admit it felt a little odd because I wasn't sure if God would speak or if it would feel like me making up something to say to myself. My seminary professor encouraged us just to try it with an open mind and ask God to speak, so I decided to go for it. I started with my name at the top of the paper and then just asked the Lord what He wanted to say to me that day.

I was surprised at how natural it felt to write what I believed God was saying to me and how I even felt it came in a different tone than the one I typically write in. A good portion of the letter is often encouragement from God about how much He loves me or how He is with me in whatever circumstance I am experiencing. He will often bring to mind scriptures that apply directly to my current struggles or questions. Sometimes I will hear a specific answer to something I have been asking Him. But my primary purpose in spending time with God is not to receive information or get answers; my principal reason is to know Him and to walk with Him. Out of this relationship will come all that I need to know for each day, including where He is leading me.

After you finish journaling, it is important to remember to submit everything back to God. To be sure, I always ask Him if I misheard or wrote anything that was not from Him and, if so, to redirect me. Just like anything else you hear from God, no matter how you hear it, it is important to test the word you've received and run it through filters, such as seeing if it lines up with Scripture, testing it through the godly counsel in your life, and examining whether you feel the peace of God about the direction you heard. I will address all these steps in more detail in the following chapters of the book. You will also have an opportunity to try two-way journaling as a part of the 40-Day Challenge.

Devo Time

A "devo time" is what I call my daily devotional time with God. That is a block of time I set aside to spend in worship, prayer, and Bible study. The simple steps I outlined in this chapter will be a core part of your devo time and help you download God's specific message for you. We will talk more about having a devo time throughout this book and give you more detailed instructions and a structure to follow in The Experiment.

The Bible is meant to propel you into conversation with God, so keep the conversation going even after your official devo time is over. Some of my best revelations have come in the middle of my day, when God drops an idea in my mind or speaks something to me in reply to what I asked Him earlier or what I read in Scripture. As you keep the communication lines open, He shows up and delights to speak!

Mark it Up!

I once heard that a Bible that is falling apart usually belongs to a person who is not, so I make it my personal goal to mark up my Bibles by highlighting, writing, and poring over their pages. In fact, every year I write my annual goals on a piece of paper and tape it in the front cover of my Bible. Every time God speaks something really specific to me or gives significant direction for my life, I write it on the back cover of my Bible.

I recommend marking up your Bibles because you can look back through the pages and see all the ways God has met you and worked in your life. God wants to build a personal history with you through His Word. When He highlights a verse or a promise, it comes alive. I like to write the date next to a passage or write down what God spoke to me through the passage so that I can remember each encounter with Him.

When I am having a difficult day or feeling distant from God, I can go back to these passages where I have already met with God and experienced triumphs. These verses often become a springboard that propels me back to Him. This takes any Bible from being God's Word and turns it into God's Word for you!

If you have not encountered God in this way, ask Him. He loves to reveal Himself to those who are hungry and speak to those who desire to hear Him. God's Word is never meant to be merely a theological book to be studied. Its primary role is to draw you closer to the Author so that you can know Him and be led by Him. Remember the story of Elijah I referenced earlier? God did not speak to Elijah in an earthquake, mighty wind, or a fire but, rather, a still, small voice. The reason why He uses a still, small voice is because He is close, and when you're close, you only need to whisper. Get to know the Word and you will draw close to the Author.

One of the analogies that God uses to explain the importance of His Word is when He compares it to bread. The children of Israel walked in the desert for forty years, and there were some pretty amazing things going on out in that desert. First, God led them with a cloud by day and a pillar of fire by night. In addition, He miraculously provided food because there's not a lot to eat in the desert. So He caused it to rain bread—manna from heaven—every day.

Exodus 16:4 says, "Then the Lord said to Moses, 'I will rain down bread from heaven for you. The people are to go out each day and gather enough for that day. In this way I will test them and see whether they will follow my instructions.'" He explained that He would do this every day to test them and see whether or not they would follow Him.

God's role was to provide, but the Israelites had a role to play: they were to gather new manna every day because it would rot if they tried to keep it overnight. God's test was simple: Either they were going to be full that day or they were going to be hungry. Either they were going to gather and consume the manna or they were going to find themselves weak, tired, and frustrated.

I believe this passage foreshadows the relationship God invites us to have with His Word. He promises to provide spiritual food for us, but there is a significant responsibility on our parts. We have to literally make the steps to research and seek God through His Word daily so that we can apply His message to our lives. The test is simple. If we get to Wednesday and we're feeling a little bit overwhelmed by life, a bit frustrated by our circumstances, or perhaps a little weary and anxious, we should honestly evaluate if we have been seeking out and applying God's message to our circumstances every day.

God's Word has sustenance that provides exactly what we need at the right time and in the right way, but we have to set aside time to seek out His message in order to find it and to receive it.

Once you have asked your questions and done your research, you are ready to move on to Steps Three and Four in the scientific method: constructing and testing your hypothesis.

CHAPTER THREE

Constructing and Testing
the Hypothesis

There are two possible outcomes: if the result confirms the hypothesis, then you've made a measurement. If the result is contrary to the hypothesis, then you've made a discovery.

—ENRICO FERMI, ITALIAN PHYSICIST [1]

Let the wise listen and add to their learning, and let the discerning get guidance.

—PROVERBS 1:5

In the scientific method, Step Three is to construct a hypothesis—an educated guess about how something will work. It is based on the question(s) asked in Step One and the research gleaned in Step Two. It is an educated guess because it is merely a prediction of the answer to the question based on your research. In your elementary school bean experiment, the hypothesis was that if you stuck a seed in some dirt, watered it daily, and exposed it to the warmth of a heat lamp, the seed would sprout and become a bean plant.

The hypothesis here is what you believe God is speaking to you. As you posed your question(s) to the Lord, listened for His voice and direction, and further discovered His direction through your research into the written Word of God, you came up with an idea of what He is speaking to you and what He desires you to do—with the expectation that your obedience to His direction will result in certain outcomes.

Before you launch out on what you believe God is speaking to you, or if you still remain uncertain of His direction—even after following Steps One and Two—I encourage you to share your hypothesis with one or two close friends. In addition to speaking through the still, small voice and His Word, another primary way God speaks is through other people. Sharing with others what you believe God is speaking to you and allowing them to give you feedback correlates with Step Four in the scientific method, which is to test your hypothesis by doing an experiment. This step is absolutely key and is one of the most missed steps in the process of hearing from God.

A scientist would never stop a science experiment at Step Three with just a hypothesis, so why do we stop here when we think we have heard from God? There are still steps left in the process that I believe help to build our confidence in what God is saying!

A Prophetic Word

My first job out of college was as youth pastor in the little town of DeRidder, Louisiana. I knew I was called to full-time ministry and desired to go to seminary, but I had no idea how I would ever pay for it. An opportunity presented itself for me to build a house, although there was no way I could afford to build a house on my $12,000-a-year youth-pastor salary, but my dad offered to cosign the loan with me.

I kept praying that God would clearly show me if it was something I should move forward with and to shut the door if it was not. On the Sunday before I needed to decide, I prayed the whole forty-five-minute drive to church about whether I was supposed to take out the loan and build the house.

I was actually leaning against doing so because I started wondering if it was wise to borrow all that money. As it turned out, the title of the sermon was "There is a Miracle in Your House." Through that message I was flooded with peace and knew that God was giving me His go-ahead to build the house. I had no idea that it would be Taryn's and my first home. The house also provided the finances for us to afford a home when we responded to God's call to move to D.C. There truly was a miracle in my house.

I knew God had clearly spoken to me through the message about something the pastor didn't even know I was asking God.

I love it when God speaks so definitively through someone else to answer a specific question I have asked Him. There have been numerous times similar to this when I have received an answer to something I was praying about through someone else. At first glance these incidences appear to be coincidences, but each time I knew it was actually God speaking directly to me and confirming His voice.

Other times God has spoken to me through someone else who's received a Word from Him for me. These are often called prophetic words, and I absolutely love it when I receive one that resonates or speaks to me right where I am. However, prophetic words are not the primary way we should seek to hear God through other people. They are usually encouraging words of affirmation of either what God is speaking or what else God could be saying.

Counsel

The most frequent and reliable way God speaks to us through others is through relationships in our lives that Scripture calls counsel or advisors. For example, Proverbs 15:22 says, "Plans fail for lack of counsel, but with many advisors they succeed." The focus of this chapter is going to be on the importance of having counsel in our lives and how we can best position ourselves to hear from Him through these intentional and God-first relationships. One of the primary roles of counsel is to test what we believe we have heard from God to see if it resonates with others.

Why do so few people prioritize seeking out counsel as a way for God to speak to them or to confirm what they believe He has already spoken? One reason is because people are afraid that their hypothesis will be proven wrong when tested. They would rather not submit the message to trusted counsel because they want to do what they want to do without other people's input. These people tend to use the phrase "God told me to do this" at alarmingly frequent rates and are not open to hearing another person's perspective if he or she disagrees with theirs. I do not think I need to elaborate on why these people are placing themselves in an unhealthy, dangerous position. Proverbs 12:15 describes them as fools because they are not seeking or heeding counsel, "The way of a fool *is* right in his own eyes but he who heeds counsel *is* wise."[2]

I had an individual come to my office a few years ago claiming to be seeking counsel. After entering the room, he sat down on my couch and proceeded to tell me God had spoken to him and that he knew what he was going to do in the situation—even though he was supposedly coming to me to seek my advice. When I asked him why he made the appointment, he said, "Well, the Bible says I am supposed to seek counsel." I asked him, "If I told you I didn't think you should move forward in the situation, would you change your mind or course of action?" He answered with a frank but adamant "no." This man was not coming to seek counsel. He was coming to communicate information in hopes that I would agree with him and he could check off what he felt was the obligatory command from God to "seek counsel."

There are many like this man who honestly do not want counsel. However, I believe the most common reason people don't seek counsel is that they have never chosen anyone to play this role in their lives. They either skip this step entirely or they end up asking a plethora of people whom they are not in a close relationship with or who do not have a biblical worldview. It is no surprise that they end up getting confused when their counsel gives different advice. They often misuse Proverbs 11:14, which says, "Where there is no counsel, the people fall; but in the multitude of counselors there is safety."[3]

Wise Counsel

Proverbs 11:14 says to seek counsel through a multitude of counselors, but when we look at the Hebrew word for counsel, we receive a vital barometer to use when selecting the people we ask. The Hebrew word for counsel translates to "wise counsel or good advice and direction," and the Hebrew word for counselors means those who "counsel or give wise advice." This verse is saying not to choose just any group of counselors, but those who give wise advice.

The Hebrew word for counsel is also a nautical term, conveying that receiving and following wise advice will help steer us in the right direction. Therefore, it is paramount to make the right choice regarding whom we choose to speak to about our lives because, as this verse reminds us, when we choose well, we will find safety.

So how do we find wise counsel? I have three preliminary questions I use as a litmus test:

Are they walking closely with God?

The first question I ask: "Are they walking closely with God?" is the most important question. Proverbs 11:14 says we need to have those who will give us wise advice, and this comes best from those who have a vibrant relationship with God and make decisions with a biblical worldview.

Having a vibrant relationship with God means they spend time with God and hear from Him. I want to receive counsel from someone who is listening to His leading, both for their lives and for my life.

I define someone with a biblical worldview as one who looks to the Word of God as their ultimate truth and authority, which means that their value system lines up with God's value system. This manifests in their lives through their personal character, their genuine love for people, and their desire to live life for what ultimately matters—eternity.

Are they walking closely with me?

The second question, "Are they walking closely with me?" is also very important because I have found that the people who can give me the best advice are the people who know me the very best. They know my strengths, weaknesses, fears, dreams, and insecurities, so they have insight into my life that others would miss. They also are praying for me on a regular basis and have a vested interest in my life, so they are trusted counselors whose words have weight and authority.

Are they able to tell me no?

The third question, "Are they able to tell me no?" is one that is often missed. If you surround yourself with those who automatically agree with you, often referred to as yes men, you are missing the whole point of seeking counsel. You need to give people permission to tell you no and take the time to listen to why they disagree with you or have reservations about your ideas. Those closest to you often have a different vantage point that is able to bring to light something you missed seeing and even save you from future trouble. Proverbs 19:20 says, "Listen to advice and accept discipline, and at the end you will be counted among the wise." Are you willing to hear advice or discipline, even when it is not what you want to hear, and take time to seriously weigh what has been shared?

Someone who was not afraid to give me straightforward advice and even provide some needed discipline in my life was Billy Hornsby. Billy was one of the founders of the Association of Related Churches (ARC), an organization that helps plant churches all over the world, who became a mentor and personal friend. He was one of the kindest, most fun-loving men you could ever meet, but he was also not afraid to speak the truth. I learned this firsthand when he came to visit DC Metro about a year after we planted the church. He evaluated every aspect of our services and of the DC Metro experience, and he gave us a C-minus. Yes, only slightly better than a D. Ouch! I admit this was a tough pill to swallow because he was a man I deeply respected and I wanted him to be impressed with the ministry we were developing in our nation's capital.

However, looking back, I am thankful for his brutal honesty, because he gave me a list of ten things he would change. For example, he said we needed to train our leaders on how to host guests because his experience of being hosted was subpar. He advised us to remove superfluous parts of the service, such as long prayers and any language that non-Christians and new believers would not understand. He also recommended adding a ten-minute guest reception at the end of each service to be able to connect with those who were new to the church.

We implemented every one of his recommendations and saw immediate fruit, especially in our guest relations. After his assessment, we were compelled to study the organizations with the best guest relations in the world to find the ones we would model ourselves after: the Ritz-Carlton, Nordstrom, and Starbucks. For example, from the Ritz we learned that you should always walk your guests to wherever they are asking directions to rather than just pointing them in the right direction. Nordstrom trains their employees to answer any question related to any department, and if they cannot answer, they will personally escort you to someone who can answer your question. After learning this, we started to train our different serving teams at church to be able to answer basic questions about other serving teams and if they could not answer the guest's questions, they were instructed to take the person to a leader on the serving team. Finally, Starbucks desires to be your "third place," where you hang out other than work and home, and after learning this we intentionally created environments and places for people to connect with one another because we want church to be their third place.

I am happy to say that when Billy returned a year later, he gave his experience at DC Metro an A. The only significant feedback he recommended on his second visit was that I take my family on a vacation because we needed some rest and quality time together. He also challenged me to intentionally invest in a relationship with another ARC church planter whose church was at a similar stage as DC Metro.

My first thought was Pastor Rob Brendle from Denver United Church. What I didn't know is that Billy had told Pastor Rob something similar. At Billy's bidding, we both began to invest in our relationship, and Rob quickly became a close friend. He actually took Billy's place on our board, as one of DC Metro's Overseers when Billy passed away. I am incredibly thankful for Billy's willingness to give me honest feedback and to challenge me because it is still bearing fruit in my life and in DC Metro today. Do you have these types of relationships in your life? If not, I believe it is God's desire to help you find them.

S.A.F.E. Relationships

A recent study indicated that the greatest statistical predictor of spiritual growth is the quantity of close Christian friends a person has in any given season of his or her life. In other words, from a statistical growth standpoint, having healthy, God-first friendships is far more important than any other Christian behavior or discipline. Peter Haas, founder and lead pastor of Substance Church in Minneapolis, elaborates on these findings, "In fact, you can preach the same quantity of God's Word at two different people, and studies show that the 'person with more friends' is the one who is 'most likely to apply it.'"[4]

This study reinforces our DC Metro small group motto: "Transformation happens best in the context of healthy, God-first relationships." We believe healthy, God-first relationships are S.A.F.E. relationships, meaning that they are:

Supportive—We are called to support and encourage one another. After all, we all need friends who will be there for us in both the good times and the hard times.

Accountable—We need people in our lives who we can be totally authentic with, who sharpen us and, no matter what, point us back to Christ.

Fun—We need people in our lives who we can enjoy and who help us live the abundant life God calls us to enjoy together.

Empowering—We are called to speak into one another's lives and help each other fulfill our God-given purpose and potential in life.

I intentionally place S.A.F.E. relationships in my life not only because they enrich my life and have helped me become who I am called to be, but also because they play the vital role of providing me trusted, godly counsel.

Supportive

The people you place as counsel should play a supportive, encouraging role in the narrative of your life. As I mentioned when I shared the three questions I ask when choosing counsel, they are people who should know you well and love you, because this gives them more authority and insight to speak into your life. They will sacrifice for you and help support you so that you can accomplish more together than you could possibly accomplish apart.

Ecclesiastes 4:9–12 describes the advantages of this type of unified, synergistic relationship:

> Two are better than one, because they have a good return for their labor. If either of them falls down, one can help the other up. But pity anyone who falls and has no one to help them up. Also, if two lie down together, they will keep warm. But how can one keep warm alone? Though one may be overpowered, two can defend themselves. A cord of three strands is not quickly broken.

This passage reminds me of Bubba's relationship with Forrest Gump when he stated, "I'm gonna lean up against you, you just lean right back against me. This way, we don't have to sleep with our heads in the mud. You know why we a good partnership, Forrest? 'Cause we be watchin' out for one another. Like brothers and stuff."[5] Our lives get real muddy when we attempt to go it alone. Jethro modeled this type of supportive relationship to Moses in Exodus 18. Even though Moses had received the best education available in Egypt, I believe he learned even more from Jethro about practical leadership. Jethro taught Moses how he could serve the people more strategically. After heeding Jethro's advice, Moses became a much better leader of the people, and a better sustainer of his own life.

Jethro knew Moses had a tendency to try to please people because Jethro understood Moses's weaknesses. Jethro told Moses there was no way Moses could continue to handle the number of people who wanted to see him every day without his growing too weary. Jethro played a vital role by speaking into Moses's life and coming up with a practical solution to an issue affecting his success as a leader. We all need people in our lives who help us know our blind spots and support us by figuring out practical ways we can overcome our current obstacles.

Accountable

The people we place as counsel also have a role of accountability. As we agree to be authentic with them and give them permission to speak into our lives, they bring great affirmation of the road ahead. The Overseers of DC Metro are some who play this role in my life because I openly share with them when I am walking through a challenge. However, the two people who play this role in the greatest way are my wife, Taryn, and my best friend, Matt. I have allowed them access to every area of my life, and have agreed to be transparent with them in any area of struggle. Although sometimes a bit humbling and even embarrassing, I have found it to also be one of the most freeing disciplines in life.

When we confess our sins to each other and share our insecurities and fears, we are actually deepening our relationship with the other person. We are showing them that they are someone we value and trust enough to share the parts of our selves that are not open to the public. I have found that transparency begets transparency, so if I open up and share first, I am also providing a safe place where they can be themselves and share openly about their shortcomings and insecurities. No matter how embarrassing or how revealing, this type of open transparency brings safety.

James 5:16 instructs, "Therefore confess your sins to each other and pray for each other so that you may be healed. The prayer of a righteous person is powerful and effective." The Greek word for "healed" in this passage can be translated as "physical healing," but it can also mean "healing of the soul." I have found both to be true in my own life, especially the healing of the soul, which is comprised of our mind, will, and emotions.

In James 5:16, we are instructed to "pray for each other," which is written in the present imperative and translates as "pray and keep on praying for each other." We are able to serve one another by being a reflection of God's heart in the midst of our brokenness and by praying for one another when we share our failures. There is something powerful that takes place as you show yourself as you really are, which leads to receiving unconditional love.

Recently, my son Isaac grabbed a book from my seminary days off my bookshelf. It was about the healing power of community called *The Safest Place on Earth*. As I began reading it again, I began to see how timely it was that Isaac should "happen" to pick up this particular book, because this action confirmed what God had been teaching me. This book provoked me to be even more transparent in my closest relationships.

In this book, Larry Crabb explains, "A central task of community is to create a safe enough place for walls to be torn down. . . . In spiritual community, people reach deep places in each other's hearts that are not often or easily reached. They openly express love and reveal fear even though they are not accustomed to that level of intimacy. When they reach a sacred place of vulnerability and authenticity, something is released. Something good begins to happen."[6]

It's amazing when we experience true Christian friendship the way Christ intended it to be. The results are altogether transformative to our souls. If you have yet to experience this—I challenge you—be vulnerable and open up to a safe person: the results will leave you desiring more.

Fun

I personally believe that the people who you place as closest counsel in your life should be those you have fun with and enjoy. I will be the first to admit that, at first glance, many pastors would not consider fun as one of their top qualifications for counsel, but I definitely recommend this quality. Most Americans have a tendency to overwork and, consequently, their lives becomes unbalanced, with their personal lives and having fun taking a backseat to their careers. I don't believe this is God's design for us, as He desires us to make life-giving relationships a top priority in our lives.

First of all, I believe you should sincerely enjoy the people you have in the closest places in your life. I have had the same best friends for almost fifteen years. We vacation together, we have dinner parties together, and we celebrate birthdays and life's other milestones together. Simply put, we have a ridiculous amount of fun together. Just as in a marriage, I believe you need to be intentional about doing activities that you enjoy together and that you need to be purposeful about having fun. I want those who are speaking into my life to know what makes my heart come alive, what makes me laugh, and what brings me the deepest joy. After all, as C. S. Lewis wrote, "Joy is the serious business of heaven."[7]

Second, I want to receive from people who are living the life that Jesus promised in John 10:10, "I have come that they may have life, and have it to the full." I purposefully seek out those who know how to live to the fullest and who help me live this carpe-diem lifestyle. Whoever said God is boring and that our lives as Christians have to be dull has not had a true revelation of Him. God is the most enjoyable being that has ever existed, and I want to be around those who remind me of this reality. After all, life and ministry are meant to be fun and fulfilling adventures with God.

Some may argue that fun is too hedonistic of a barometer, but I have found the most profound joy actually comes from serving Jesus, doing life with other believers, and being a part of others' lives being transformed. This is the type of fun I am talking about and what I seek to share with those who play the role of my closest friends and advisors. I think we could all use a little more fun in our lives. After all, walking out God's call is meant to be an enjoyable group project.

Empowering

The counsel in your life should also be empowering. We talked about biblical accountability earlier. We tend to focus on areas of sin or weakness when we think of accountability, but true biblical accountability also includes empowerment. You hold the people closest in your life accountable to the dreams that are in their hearts and to living out the gifts and passions you see in their lives. You hold them accountable to be who God has called them to be, and you will do anything you can to empower them or to help them fulfill their calling.

Empowering is one of my favorite roles to play with those who are on our executive leadership team. A couple of years ago we went out to lunch as a lead team. Dr. Joseph Umidi, the current dean of Regent University's School of Divinity and one of our DC Metro Overseers, shared with us what he believed was the main reason why DC Metro had grown at a significant rate yet remained spiritually healthy: our relationships with each other. Dr. Umidi called our relationships our secret sauce because they are what the Holy Spirit flows through to reveal the deep, unconditional love of God.

I began to unpack Dr. Umidi's statement as I looked at the people around the table. I have known most of the members of the lead team for over a decade. We have walked together both through each other's trials as well as our victories. We know each other's weaknesses and vulnerabilities, but we also know how to call forth the best in each other. We know beyond a shadow of a doubt that we are for each other and that we are better together than we would be apart. I believe that God desires these types of relationships in each of our lives. C. S. Lewis explains:

> In friendship . . . we think we have chosen our peers. In reality a
> few years' difference in the dates of our births, a few more miles
> between certain houses, the choice of one university instead of
> another . . . the accident of a topic being raised or not raised at a
> first meeting—any of these chances might have kept us apart. But,

for a Christian, there are, strictly speaking, no chances. A secret master of ceremonies has been at work. Christ, who said to the disciples, "You have not chosen me, but I have chosen you," can truly say to every group of Christian friends, "You have not chosen one another but I have chosen you for one another."[8]

I know God strategically placed each of the people who are in the closest places in my life, but it has taken intentionality on my part to invest in these relationships. If you do not already have these S.A.F.E relationships in your life, I believe God wants to help you develop them. It is a strategic way that He wants to speak to you. If you do have these relationships, I encourage you to continue to invest in them and ask God to help you recognize His voice through them. They are truly your greatest assets in this life.

Bonds and Boats

When I was in seminary, I was honored when my dad, someone I deeply respect, asked me for counsel when he told me he found a sailboat he wanted to buy. After many years of casually looking at boats, this particular boat had captured his attention enough that he asked me to pray about whether he should buy it—he was unsure if he should spend a large amount of money on a recreational expense.

It is important to mention that my dad is extremely thrifty, and he actually had the money in a savings account from an insurance reimbursement he had received years earlier when his old boat was destroyed in a Louisiana hurricane. In my mind, I thought he should buy the boat because he has always had a passion for sailing, and he had the money sitting in a bank account. However, because I knew how unlikely it was for my frugal dad to buy anything he considered frivolous, I told him I would pray that God would confirm whether or not he should buy the boat. Little did I know how incredibly God would answer that prayer.

When I entered the campus prayer chapel—a routine of mine each day before hitting the books in the library—I had two main requests to lift up to God. The first was my dad's boat, and the second was my need for additional finances for living expenses while I was in seminary. At the time I had a series of part-time jobs, but it was still a stretch each month to pay all my bills. My roommate, Matt, and I were living off of hot dogs and mac and cheese, so I decided I would ask God for help.

After about half an hour talking with God, and right before I was getting ready to leave, I heard God say, *Sell the bonds and I'll give him the boat.* This phrase was honestly baffling to me because I did not know what bonds He was talking about—even though I knew it was His voice.

While I was asking God what He meant, I suddenly remembered that my parents had told me years earlier that they had purchased savings bonds for me when I was born. I also remembered that a week earlier my mom had sent me an old accordion file containing papers and documents from my childhood. When I'd received this file, I'd stuck it in my closet and given no thought to what it contained.

I decided to skip my time in the library that afternoon to go on a little adventure with God. On my drive home, I wondered if that old file could possibly contain the savings bonds my parents had bought for me a quarter of a century ago. I was thrilled when I pulled the accordion file from the closet to find a dusty manila envelope with the savings bonds that had matured only one month prior. However, nothing could have prepared me for what else I pulled out of that same envelope: there was a brochure for a sailboat that I had picked up at a marina in Louisiana and placed in the file years earlier. I know . . . what are the odds? Well, it gets even better. I pulled out the brochure for the sailboat to find out it was for a 1997 Hunter twenty-five-foot sailboat, which was the exact make, model, and year that my dad was looking at! In my left hand, I was holding the savings bonds, and in my right hand, I was holding the brochure. I was so blown away I could hardly contain myself at the specificity and goodness of God.

The phrase "Sell the bonds and I'll give him the boat" reverberated in my head, as now it made perfect sense. Of course, I immediately called my dad and told him I felt very confident that God wanted him to buy the boat. God knew it was hard for my dad to buy things for himself, so He wanted to do something so overt that no one could doubt—not even my dad—that God wanted him to buy a boat. God knew I was struggling financially and led me to the bonds right after they matured at the exact time I was in need of finances.

As my father sought out my counsel on his desire to purchase a boat, God confirmed his decision to me as I prayed and through the unique circumstances of the bonds and the boat brochure. Not only was I able to affirm his decision in my counsel, but God used the situation to meet my financial needs.

As incredible as it was for my dad to get the sailboat he had been dreaming about and for me to get the financial resources I needed, we received something far more valuable that day. We heard the voice of God in an undeniable way, which became a powerful reminder of how much He loves us and how He is involved in the intricate details of our lives. We still marvel at the kindness of God and how we believe He had been planning that surprise for us since my parents had first bought the bonds twenty-five years earlier.

Choosing Your Counsel

By seeking counsel in life as you attempt to hear from God, you will truly fulfill the scientific method of the practical science of hearing God's voice. Testing your hypothesis by inviting others to weigh in on what you believe God is speaking to you will prove to be a final confirmation or a S.A.F.E. redirection as His voice is clarified.

In the 40-Day Challenge, we are going to ask you to share what God speaks to you as you spend thirty minutes with Him each day for forty days. In preparation, think of one relationship you have that is a good candidate for being your wise counsel. Remember, I define wise counsel as a person who is walking closely with God and with you, and who will not be afraid to tell you no if they do not agree with what you believe God is saying.

Is the individual you have in mind a S.A.F.E. relationship? Are they supportive, will they provide accountability, are they fun and empowering? If your answer to all the above questions is yes, give them a call and schedule a time to meet.

During your meeting, share with your friend the purpose of The Experiment.

+ Give them a summary of *Hearing from God* (or, better yet, give them a copy) and share how you are applying the steps of the scientific method to learning to hear and discern the voice of God.

+ Explain where they fit into the process and, as a person you trust, you can share what you believe God is speaking to you.

+ Tell them the definition you learned of wise counsel and what a S.A.F.E. relationship is. Tell them why you picked them for the role.

+ If they agree to fill the role, pray together for God to bless the relationship, and give them wisdom and discernment.

+ Share with them what you have been asking God and the answers you believe God has spoken to you through your prayer and study.

+ Remember, no counsel you choose will give you perfect advice or hear from the Lord perfectly. If your counsel does not believe you should move forward in what you shared, it is worth investing some significant time in prayer and asking them to continue to pray, too.

+ Don't do all the talking. After you have spoken, allow your friend the freedom to ask questions and share their ideas and counsel.

You have asked God your question(s) and done research in the Word of God—looking for answers to your questions or confirmation of the answers you already received. You have submitted your hypothesis of what you believe God is speaking to you to trusted counsel from other individuals. Now it's time to move on to Step Five of the scientific method: analyzing and drawing a conclusion about what you believe God has spoken.

CHAPTER FOUR

Analysis and Conclusion

The only relevant test of the validity of a hypothesis is comparison of prediction with experience.

—MILTON FRIEDMAN, ECONOMIST [1]

Do not be anxious about anything, but in every situation, by prayer and petition, with thanksgiving, present your requests to God. And the peace of God, which transcends all understanding, will guard your hearts and your minds in Christ Jesus.

—PHILIPPIANS 4:6–7

Step Five of the scientific method is to analyze the data and draw a conclusion. The data is the record of what happened during the experiment. Once a scientist has completed his or her experiment, they collect and analyze the data to see if it supports the original hypothesis. Many times scientists find that their original hypothesis could not be supported by the data. Based on what they have learned from their experiments, the scientists will develop a new hypothesis. This starts the scientific method process over again.

Thomas Edison had a hypothesis of what it would take to create the lightbulb. He made over a thousand attempts and filled over forty thousand pages of notes before he found the missing piece that led him to his invention. Edison was searching for the right material for the filament, the little wire inside the lightbulb. " 'Before I got through,' Edison recalled, 'I tested no fewer than 6,000 vegetable growths, and ransacked the world for the most suitable filament material.' "[2] His attempts included coconut fiber, fishing line, and even hairs from a friend's beard, before Edison finally figured out to use carbonized bamboo for the filament.[3]

Patent number 223,898 was given to Edison's electric bulb, which was one of 1,093 patents accredited to him.[4] Edison reflected on his pièce de résistance, "The electric light has caused me the greatest amount of study and has required the most elaborate experiments. . . . We are striking it big in the electric light, better than my vivid imagination first conceived. Where this thing is going to stop, Lord only knows."[5] Thankfully Edison did not give up on searching for the missing piece.

Edison was one of my middle-school heroes. As I shared earlier, I incessantly dreamed of one day having a patent in my name. In fact, in my quest to win at a science fair, I entered four different fairs over the course of four years trying the same experiment with magnets. Each time, I attempted to make a metal ball levitate by wrapping coils around nails to create a magnetic pull strong enough to keep the ball floating in midair.

Each year it was an epic fail, so I hypothesized that I needed more power and tried to add a stronger magnetic pull each successive year. Ironically, even though my science experiment failed again and again, my final year I still won the science fair for explaining why my hypothesis was wrong. My missing piece was power. I am sorry to say that, unlike Edison, I did not have the tenacity to keep trying after the fourth failed attempt, so the missing piece remained missing.

Finding the "Missing Peace"

Have you ever had a missing piece that you desperately needed to make something work? Nothing can be more frustrating than missing a piece to a puzzle or the final part of a solution to an issue.

When it comes to hearing the voice of God and discerning which direction to step, I have found that there is a final piece that simply cannot remain missing, which is the peace of God. One of the first questions I ask myself when I am contemplating taking a step in a certain direction is: "Do I have peace?" If I believe I have heard God through His still, small voice, His Word, or through counsel, I always test it by asking myself whether or not I feel peace.

At first the litmus test of whether or not I feel peace about the situation or direction can seem too subjective or too dependent on mood. That is, until you understand that the biblical definition of peace is much more than a feeling and is one of the primary ways He confirms where He is leading you. As the next step, analyzing the data and drawing a conclusion is used to evaluate the direction we have received from the Lord, but at the end of the day I do not move forward without His peace.

A Biblical Understanding of Peace

The word *peace* is mentioned four hundred times throughout Scripture and has several different connotations. The first connotation describes a believer's state of reconciliation with God because of what Jesus did on the cross. Romans 5:1 says, "Therefore, since we have been justified through faith, we have peace with God through our Lord Jesus Christ."

The second connotation of peace describes the type of relationship God desires us to have with others. Talking about this type of relational peace, Romans 12:18 states "as far as it depends on you, live at peace with everyone."

The third connotation of peace is the one that we are going to be focusing on in this chapter. It is listed as the third fruit of the Spirit in Galatians 5:22 and is described in Philippians 4:7: "The peace of God, which transcends all understanding, will guard your hearts and your minds in Christ Jesus."

The Greek word for peace means "harmony or tranquility." But as Philippians 4:7 explains, this peace is supernatural and beyond rational comprehension. This Greek word should be understood as "not just freedom from trouble, but everything that makes for a man's highest good,"[6] and relates to the Hebrew word for peace, *shalom*, which has a basic meaning of "totality or completeness including fulfillment, maturity, soundness, and wholeness."[7]

Let's look at a few other verses that describe this supernatural peace to further understand this gift that God gives to believers as we submit ourselves to His leadership. Isaiah 26:3 says: "You will keep in perfect peace those whose minds are steadfast, because they trust in you." In other words, peace is promised for those who trust in Him. Isaiah 55:12 explains "you shall go out in joy, and be led forth in peace." Joy and peace are gifts from the Lord as we follow Him. In John 14:27, Jesus again promises His supernatural peace to believers, "Peace I leave with you; my peace I give you. I do not give you as the world gives. Do not let your hearts be troubled and do not be afraid." It is evident that this peace does not come from the absence of trials or problems but, rather, comes from the presence of God no matter what you are walking through or where you are going.

What about my emotions?

Have you noticed that your emotions are not particularly trust-worthy? In fact, depending on what is happening in your life, your emotions can be like a roller coaster—way up one moment and way down the next, not to mention when they take you on a ride around in loops. While your feelings are a normal part of your human nature, and not to be suppressed or denied, be careful that you don't let them take the lead in your life, as they can take you places you don't want to go.

When I talk about the peace of God, I am not talking about your feelings. The peace of God is something that transcends your human emotions and rational comprehension. There is an old gospel song that talks about God giving peace in the midst of the storm. The idea is that in the middle of turmoil and chaos (the storm) God can give a supernatural peace that everything will somehow be all right. Your rollercoaster of emotions in the storm may include fear, anxiety, or dread, but somehow the peace of God overrides all the emotions and gives you the grace to trust in Him.

While the peace of God can have a calming effect on your emo-tions, it is not given to you through your emotions, but by the Holy Spirit to your human spirit. That's why Philippians 4:6–7 tells us not to be anxious about anything (emotion), but to tell God our needs and thank Him for meeting our needs (spirit to Spirit communication with God). The result will be His peace—deposited in our human spirit—guarding our hearts and minds.

If you haven't completely sorted out the difference between your emotions and His peace, don't worry. Your ability to discern between them will increase as you grow in your relationship to Him.

The Peace of God Guides Us

So how does peace relate to God's guidance? Colossians 3:15 gives us further insight: "let the peace of God rule in your hearts."[8] In the Amplified Bible, the word rule is defined as "act as an umpire." Just as an umpire decides whether a play is safe, fair, or good, so the peace of God is to act as an umpire in the decisions we make. The Good News Translation of this same verse says, "The peace that Christ gives is to guide you in the decisions you make."

Sometimes I know God has been leading me to make decisions that do not seem completely logical, but they are accompanied by what I can only describe as supernatural peace. I felt God's presence strongly with me, which manifested as the peace that passes all understanding that Paul referred to in Philippians 4:7.

One of these times was when God called Taryn and me to move across the country to start DC Metro Church. I was an associate pastor at an incredible church I loved: Celebration Church in Jacksonville, Florida. Taryn was also on staff working in the women's ministry. We thoroughly enjoyed our roles and relationships in the church. We had known for many years that God was calling us to plant a church in the D.C. metro area one day in the future, but we did not know when He would send us, so we became very rooted in Celebration.

In November 2006, Taryn and I both began to strongly feel it was time. We met with our lead pastors and dear friends, Stovall and Kerri Weems, who agreed with us. We all felt God's indescribable peace, even though it made us sad to think about not doing life and ministry together. It certainly did not seem logical to leave. Our son Isaac was only a year old at the time of our move, and we had just found out that Taryn was pregnant with our second son Josiah.

We were also leaving people we loved and secure jobs in a phenomenal church—and for what—to launch out into the unknown with no income and a growing family to support? Not exactly what most financial advisors would recommend, but the remarkable part is that we felt an unwavering, supernatural peace along with the peace that came through my pastor's counsel and support. Now don't get me wrong—Taryn and I would look at each other sometimes and ask if we were crazy. However, even in the midst of our questioning, we felt an undeniable peace—a peace that truly passed all our understanding.

I have learned that unless God's presence goes with me, I do not want to go; and if His presence is leading me, then I do not want to stay. I have found that His peace is a very helpful litmus test to see if He is initiating a move, ultimately because I want to know that He is going with me.

In Exodus 33:15, Moses expressed a similar desire when God was calling him to a foreign land. He wanted to make sure the Lord understood that the only way he was going was if God went with him: "If your presence does not go with us, do not send us up from here." I felt the exact same way when we were leaving Florida, but the peace both Taryn and I felt was confirmation that God's presence was with us and that it was He who was sending us. As we stepped out in obedience, God proved to be faithful every step of the way, and He met all our needs as we responded to His leading.

Another time God called us to step out in faith prompted by His peace was when DC Metro was moving into our first permanent facility, 1100 N Fayette Street in Alexandria, Virginia. We had been meeting in the movie theater for more than two years, and we really wanted to find a building that could become our permanent church home. On Easter Sunday morning in 2009, I was driving my normal route from Starbucks to the movie theater that we called home, when directly in my path I stumbled upon a building that was for lease. I immediately fell in love with the building, as I could picture it as a church where thousands of people would encounter God and be changed in His presence.

I began to pursue leasing this building, but I was extremely discouraged when I heard the price. After some quick mental math, I realized that our church income would have to double to afford the building. In my rational, business mind, that was an immediate no. However, to my surprise, I had an incredibly strong peace about the building. I began to seek counsel with our Overseers and our leadership team. To my astonishment again, every single one said they felt peace, too, and thought we should lease the building.

Even though part of me was quite nervous, the peace we felt was stronger, so we signed the lease to move into the building. I shared in an earlier chapter that the month we signed the lease, our church income doubled! God came through for us in a way that confirmed that His hand was definitely upon our bold step of faith. We experienced firsthand what Paul was referring to in Romans 15:13: "May the God of hope fill you with all joy and peace as you trust in him, so that you may overflow with hope by the power of the Holy Spirit."

When God is guiding you in a decision or path that does not seem logical or causes you to step outside of your comfort zone, He gives you His peace to remind you, just as He told Moses in Exodus 33:14, "My presence will go with you."

What about the really tough times?

Life is often difficult. God never promised us that every day would be easy. We face circumstances where our world is being shaken, where challenges and conflicts leave us numb and without peace, and the human emotional response is fear, sorrow, pain, or any number of other feelings. Sometimes the tough seasons in life are due to our bad choices, other people's bad choices, or even the devil's attack, but regardless of the cause of the trial, God promises to walk through those times with us.

Jesus is our best example of someone who endured tremendous difficulties. The will of God for His life was full of conflict—with religious and political leaders, in confrontations with demons, and, the ultimate, His death on the Cross. We know that His humanity caused Him to experience the full range of our human emotions—and He struggled. In the garden of Gethsemane, He told the disciples that He was "deeply distressed and troubled. 'My soul is overwhelmed with sorrow to the point of death'" (Mark 14:33–34). He prayed three separate times, asking God to remove the cup of suffering that He was about to experience. Luke's version of the story tells us that Jesus was in anguish, praying so hard His sweat was like drops of blood falling to the ground (Luke 22:44). That is some serious praying. But while Jesus was honest with His emotions, His prayer was ultimately one of submission to the will of His Father: "yet not my will, but yours be done" (Luke 22:42).

Did Jesus experience a supernatural peace that surpassed His raging emotions? The Bible is silent about that. What we do know is that after He had wrestled with His emotions in prayer—three times—He was ready to move forward in the will of God (the scourging, mocking, and the agony of the Cross). My point? When you are called to difficult circumstances in life where a natural peace is lacking, deal honestly with your emotions before God, submit yourself fully to the will of God, and move forward in the will of God. As you do that, trust that God can and will deposit a supernatural peace in your spirit that will surpass the thoughts in your mind and your roller-coaster emotions.

Losing and Regaining Your Peace

One question I am often asked is what to do if you had peace at one point, and then you lose it. Peace gives us an initial green light to take a first step, but sometimes we lose our peace along the way. There are different reasons we can lose our peace. We may have let fear creep in so that we are no longer being led by faith but rather by our emotions and insecurities. If this is the case, don't derail the process but, instead, go back to the place you first had peace.

This is exactly what happened to me when we were buying our first house in the D.C. area. We found a neighborhood we loved in the school district we wanted for our kids, so we began the search. One morning during that season, I was reading Ephesians 5, when I felt the Holy Spirit highlight verse 25: "Husbands, love your wives, just as Christ loved the church and gave Himself up for her." This is a sweet, sentimental-sounding verse that is read at many weddings, but I have been walking with the Lord long enough to know that when God highlights a verse like this, it is often because He is going to give me an opportunity to walk it out.

I was right. Almost immediately after reading that verse, I sensed the still, small voice of God whisper to let Taryn pick out the house we would buy. I consented to this prompting, but I must admit I was feeling rather prideful about what a good husband I was to let her choose the house. I felt like I deserved a big pat on the back. One of my passions is picking, purchasing, and renovating houses, but I was going to obey the passage in Ephesians and lay down my life and choices for my wife.

Taryn was elated when I told her she could pick the house. She quickly found a ranch-style house in our favorite neighborhood, but as soon as we pulled up to tour the house, I completely lost my peace. The landscaping was ridiculously overgrown. When we stepped inside, the house reeked of a foul odor. I am still not quite sure what to say about the seventies wallpaper or decor. Not to mention there was a dripping sound coming from the basement. I went downstairs to check it out only to find chains hanging from the ceiling. My immediate thought was we must have stumbled upon an ax-murderer hangout!

I looked over at Taryn to give her the *let's get out of here* look only to find my wife's eyes lit up. I thought, *Uh-oh, I know that look . . . she likes it.* My wife is an incredible visionary, and she began to envision our future home, saying, "David, we can blow this wall out and this wall out and we can renovate this area." I must confess, at that point all I could see were dollar signs flashing before my eyes. With each new project she proposed, my peace seemed to dissipate further and further at an alarming rate.

I began to dialogue with the Lord. *I can't believe she likes this house! The renovations she wants to do will cost a small fortune, and the house already costs more than it is worth, in my opinion. This does not feel peaceful!* The Lord asked me when the last time I had peace was. I thought back to when God spoke to me though Ephesians 5 and I then told Taryn she could pick the house. I quickly realized that I had tried to take control of picking the house again, when the last time God had spoken to me was to let Taryn choose. I repented and released the decision back to Taryn, and immediately my peace came rushing back. I was still not happy about the house and did not think it was the best deal, but I had peace that God was with us in the decision.

Taryn had no idea of the internal dialogue I had just had with the Lord, but she turned to me and said, "I don't think we should buy this house." My wife is a savvy businesswoman, and when she crunched the numbers, she concluded that it was overpriced. "I love the house. I have a vision for it, but I don't think the numbers make sense," she said. Secretly, I was thrilled. End of story . . . or so I thought.

The next day Taryn was back on the multiple listing service, and she realized the owners of the ranch-style house had dropped the price by seventy thousand dollars. We prayed about it again and both felt a green light and tremendous peace. All the qualities I hadn't liked about the house at first were cosmetic and easily altered, particularly because we were able to invest the money from the price drop into the needed renovations. A number of blessings resulted in following God's direction in Ephesians 5:25, but one of my favorites is how Taryn and I discovered renovating houses was a new hobby we could enjoy together. We had previously struggled to find a joint hobby, as she loves to work out and cook delicious meals from scratch (which I enjoy eating), and my hobbies are more outdoorsy, like hunting and fishing. While we were pretending to be Chip and Joanna Gaines from one of our favorite HGTV shows, *Fixer Upper,* we connected with each other in a new way, and our marriage was strengthened as a result. The house became a home where we had many happy memories. When we sold it, we even gained a significant profit. In the end, this became yet another personal testimony of the wisdom of following God's peace and how to regain it even when you lose it.

God's Redemption

I have had to follow this process of restoring peace in my own life countless times, but I have found that even when we step off course, God loves to draw us back and brings the needed redemption. There is no place that I have seen this more clearly than in my relationship with my wife. We were engaged—twice.

I met Taryn at a college conference in Baton Rouge, Louisiana, and was immediately drawn to her. I prayed with my prayer partner for six weeks for the opportunity to run into her again and ask her out. When I saw her at the business school, my fraternity brother asked whom she was dating. I thought to myself, *me.* Okay, maybe I really wasn't there at that moment, but when my fraternity brother left, I went over to her and asked her out, and to my surprise she said yes. On our first date, I talked to her about my dream of one day starting a church in the D.C. area. She shared that she, too, had dreams of doing something great for God. My heart felt an abundance of peace, as I sensed that she could be the one.

Fast-forward three years later to a broken engagement with Taryn. Confusion and hurt usurped the peace that had previously filled my heart. Hindsight is always 20/20, but I now see that I had allowed myself to be too influenced by the counsel of one person, who was against us getting married. This person was not close to either of us—hence the need for my counsel in the previous chapter. This person's perspective had triggered my own doubts as well as Taryn's, which caused both of us to pull away from each other and ultimately call off our wedding.

After we ended our engagement, I didn't talk with Taryn for almost a year, until I decided to call and check on her after the 9/11 tragedy. She then came to visit the graduate school I was attending in Virginia Beach as a prospective student, and we quickly realized we still had feelings for each other. Peace came flooding back, and within a few months we were engaged again.

Testing Counsel

Taryn and I got some negative counsel from a source that we didn't have a S.A.F.E. relationship with, bringing doubts about our relationship and leading us to break off our engagement—the first time. Unfortunately, we did not weigh the advice we were receiving and allowed it to influence our decisions.

Even when you have the most trusted counselors in your life and you receive the best counsel—you are still responsible to weigh their advice. Thessalonians 5:20-21 says: "Do not treat prophecies with contempt, but test them all and hold onto that which is good." All prophecies (words of encouragement, comfort, or direction) and advice from others need to be weighed. What is the spirit in which the advice is given? What are the consequences of following the advice—where will it lead?

Sometimes the only way to weigh the counsel of others is the test of time. Not discounting what has been spoken to you, but holding it lightly before God until He confirms the advice, or proves it wrong. You and I are to be open to counsel, but we are not to roll over and accept everything someone speaks over us, or to us—even godly people. God calls us to be responsible, testing words and holding to that which is good.

We now understand that the confusion we were feeling that had caused us to break off our engagement was not actually the lack of God's peace. The peace was just buried underneath all of the other soulful emotions that we allowed to dictate our choices. God, in His mercy, allowed us to be reunited, and we were married the next summer. One of Taryn's favorite parts of our story is that when she went to a bridal boutique in Baton Rouge to pick out a second dress, they told her they still had her original dress in the back with her name on it. The dress should have been returned over a year earlier, but the lady in the store forgot to send it back. We truly believe that God was saving the dress because He knew that our story was not over, only delayed.

I share this part of our story to remind you that we don't always hear God perfectly and sometimes we inadvertently step off course. We can trust that when we do, God will draw us back. I will say that as Romans 8:28 reminds us, God redeems and works all things together for good. During our year apart, we both drew even closer to God, which not only deepened our walk with Him but also gave us a stronger foundation for our marriage. Hearing God and walking with Him is first and foremost about having a willing heart that is seeking to follow Him. As we seek to follow Him, we analyze the data He gives us through His voice, His Word, His counsel through others, and His peace in order to draw a conclusion on what He is saying and where He is leading.

What if God doesn't answer my questions?

I have learned over the years that although God desires a relationship with each of us and wants us to continually approach Him with our questions and requests, He doesn't always give us the answers in the exact moment we ask. There are a few reasons why He may delay:

+ *You ask amiss.* James 4:3 says: "You ask and do not receive, because you ask amiss, that you may spend it on your pleasures." Why would a loving heavenly Father give you something, or answer a question about something that is not ultimately good for you? Oftentimes we don't even realize we are asking amiss and that what we are asking for is actually not God's best for us.

+ *The timing is not right.* I believe this is the most common reason we don't get answers to our requests. God sees the bigger picture of the universe and your life. In theological terms we call that His omniscience—He sees and knows all! Your pleas for something are based on your limited perspective. While your motives may be valid, there may be other factors that you do not presently understand that need to fall in place before God answers.

+ *God reserves His answers to some questions.* We need to trust the mystery and sovereignty of God. Sometimes we ask great questions like "Why won't you heal my friend of cancer?," yet we don't get a clear response. I encourage you to continue to seek God while trying not to get frustrated about the apparent lack of an answer. Deuteronomy 29:29 says: "The secret things belong to the Lord our God, but the things revealed belong to us and to our children forever, that we may follow all the words of this law."

We can trust that God will make known to us what
we need to know when we need to know it.

If He doesn't answer your specific question, ask Him to give you a word—any word, idea, thought, or verse. Keep an open mind so that He can speak to you about any topic that is on His heart. Be willing to have Him reveal if you are asking amiss, or the timing is not right, or if He's waiting for you to ask a different question first. Be open to the sources through which God will speak to you. He may be trying to answer your question, but He might be doing so in a way that is new to you. Remember, as Amos 3:7 says: He loves to share His secrets with His people, so keep seeking Him and trusting that He will reveal what you need to know when you need to know it. I have found that hearing from God is like an incredible treasure hunt where He gives you the next "clue" in His perfect timing.

How to Find Peace

If you are in a place where you are in need of peace, or if you once had peace but you lost it, here are a few actions that will help you find the supernatural peace God desires to give you.

Pray

Be completely honest before God. He wants you to tell Him what you are feeling anxious or unsure about and present your requests to Him. This is a necessary catalyst for the peace that Paul refers to in Philippians 4:6–7: "Do not be *anxious* about anything, but in every situation, by prayer and petition, with thanksgiving, present your requests to God. And the peace of God, which transcends all understanding, will guard your hearts and your minds in Christ Jesus" (emphasis mine). If you previously had peace, ask Him to help you retrace your steps back to that place, so you can release whatever you have picked up in the process that has made you question his guidance.

Release to God

This is typically the hardest but most important step. Sometimes it is called laying it on the altar, because you are fully releasing it to the Lord. When you have anxiety, pressure, or stress, it is typically because you are still trying to be in control. A good litmus test to see if you have fully given something over to God is if you sense His peace after the release. If you are still experiencing restless nights and confusion, you are most likely still holding on to the burden. 1 Peter 5:6–7 instructs, "Humble yourselves, therefore, under God's mighty hand, that He may lift you up in due time. Cast all your anxiety on him because he cares for you." His care is always most obvious when your trust is at its fullest.

Trust God's Leadership

When you have given God full control, it is then important to fully trust His leadership and His timing. God promises throughout His Word that He will guide you. Proverbs 3:5–6 says, "Trust in the Lord with all your heart and lean not on your own understanding. In all your ways submit to him, and He will make your paths straight." When you release what you had previously been holding on to, you will find not only does He flood you with His peace, but new doors of opportunity open. Why? Because He knows you can be trusted to trust Him again and again.

If you've asked God the questions on your heart, searched in His Word for answers or confirmation of what you believe He has spoken to you, and shared those answers with trusted counsel, hopefully you have experienced the final confirmation He gives through His peace about what He is saying. If not, don't be discouraged. Check out the text box in this chapter entitled "What if God Doesn't Answer My Questions?" Then wait until all the confirmations line up: His voice, His Word, His confirmation through trusted counsel, and His peace.

If all the confirmations did line up, then you are ready for Step Six in the practical science: Communicating Your Results.

CHAPTER FIVE

Communicating Your Results

If you can't explain it simply, you don't understand it well enough.

—Albert Einstein

Come! Listen, all you who are loyal to God! I will declare what He has done for me.

Psalm 66:16 NET

No experiment is complete without Step Six of the scientific method: communicating your results. For my science fair projects I created display boards that showed my hypothesis, research, experiments, and the results. Professional scientists will publish their final reports in scientific journals or present their findings at scientific symposiums.

In our practice of hearing God's voice, the final step is to tell someone what God has done in your life. As you listen for His voice, research His Word, listen to His counsel through others, and experience His peace (or lack thereof), confirming what God was saying, tell somebody! Let them know what God has done in your life, and encourage them that He can and will do the same in theirs. This is a critical part that is often missed.

Your Testimony

One of the primary reasons I wrote this book was to remind you that God wants to speak to you and that He wants to move in your life. In the Old Testament the word *testimony* comes from the Hebrew root word *uwd*, which means "to repeat, return, or do it again." As you hear other people's testimonies of how God has moved in their lives, you are reminded that your God is a God who loves to repeat Himself. As you hear stories of God moving and bringing breakthrough in someone's life, your faith is strengthened to believe God is going to move and bring breakthrough in your life, too.

Revelation 19:10 states: "the testimony of Jesus is the Spirit of prophecy."[1] I believe every time we testify of God's goodness or share a testimony of how He has spoken to us or moved in our lives, we are essentially prophesying to others what He wants to do in their lives as they partner with Him. We are preparing the atmosphere for another move of God because testimony carries with it the power of hope and change. If we speak out of our experience in God, we are not just giving information, we are providing proof that He is true to His promises, He sincerely cares about the details of our lives, and He wants to bless us. It seems only natural that we would invite others to believe that God will move again and that they, too, can experience the power of transformation!

This book contains numerous stories of how God has moved in my life and how hearing His voice has profoundly shaped and directed its course. These testimonies continue to be a catalyst for faith and trust in my own walk with God because I am reminded how He has showed up for me time and time again. As I was writing these stories, I realized there are some updates to communicate about DC Metro's story, which I've done in the next section. I am reminded of the wisdom of following His voice and how one step of obedience can set the course for years and years of good fruit if we stay connected to Him. This is the economy of God in action—any step of obedience on our part can be used to position us for the "immeasurably more" (Ephesians 3:20) He wants to do in and through us, as we align with His bigger purpose. So let me communicate the results of what God has done!

DC Metro's Testimony

Little did I know that saying yes to the vision to plant a life-giving church in the D.C. metro area in 1998 would set the trajectory of my life to be a part of all the incredible blessings we have received as a church family. The ripple effect of that original yes has included: over ten thousand people committing their lives to the Lord since 2007; countless lives encountering God's goodness as marriages have been restored; people finding authentic community in what has been called one of the loneliest cities in America; and many discovering how to hear His voice more clearly as they walk with Him toward their destinies.

As I have shared, it has not always been easy, because God's timing has been very different from mine. In my mind, I was ready to move to D.C. to start a church in 1998. Looking back, I'm very thankful that was not God's timing because, in reality, I wasn't ready. I have found that God will often give you a vision years before He gives you the green light for the vision.

For example, I shared with you in chapter 2 that God gave me a vision for the property next door in 2010, but it has taken nearly five years for that door to open. It took almost two years for the car rental company that was leasing the building to move out—a move of God because they had been in the building for thirty years. It took another year and a half for our plans to be approved, and there were many times along the way where it looked as though we were going to be denied access. All the while, I kept believing that God was going to bring it to pass at "an appointed time" and reminding myself "though it linger, wait for it, it will certainly come and not delay" (Habakkuk 2:3).

I am encouraged to share with you that DC Metro moved into this building located next door in December 2015. This building allowed us to double the number of seats available at our weekend services, allowing twice as many people the opportunity to encounter God in a real, relevant, and enjoyable environment. This also allowed us to turn our previous sanctuary into what we call the Metro Kids building, doubling our capacity to reach the next generation.

In chapter 1, I told you about the vision God gave me in 2005 for seventeen campuses in the D.C. metro area. I am excited to tell you we recently launched our third campus in Woodbridge, Virginia. God had clearly instructed us to take Virginia first. As we sought God on that phrase *Take Virginia first*, He helped me understand it further. I thought about the connotation of the word *take* and how it typically implies that it will not be an arduous battle. For example, when I hold a Lego car in my hand and tell my son Josiah to take it, all he has to do is step forward and grab it. Once I have instructed him to take it, he does not have to wrestle it out of my hands or convince me to give it to him. I had a similar sense about what God was saying for the next several campuses we would launch in Virginia. I believe God was telling us that as we continued to walk with Him, these campuses in Virginia would have His favor resting upon them. He would provide the finances, the right location, the right leaders, and He would draw the people He desired to be a part of each campus.

Launching the first two campuses in Alexandria and Fairfax were more taxing and felt like an uphill battle, but we felt like we had the wind at our backs when we launched the Woodbridge campus. I believe this will be the case for the next several campuses we launch in Virginia, as we continue to heed His direction. This is a reminder that there are different seasons in God's workings, and some are more challenging than others. But no matter what season you are in, it is important to stand on the Word God has spoken to you.

In the beginning seasons of my church, I stood on the Word I first received in 1998 and reminded God that He called us to D.C. to plant a life-giving, multicultural church in the nation's capital. When we were experiencing difficulties finding a location to launch our second campus, year after year, I stood on God's Word to me that there would be seventeen campuses in the area and reminded Him that a multisite church was His idea. As we launched our third campus and now are in the process of looking for our fourth campus in Virginia, I regularly remind myself that He has commissioned us to take Virginia first and where He guides, He provides. The multisite vision is becoming a reality as we follow God's voice where He leads.

What has God spoken to you in previous seasons that you can stand on in this season? If you do not have anything that you know He spoke, spend some time this week listening for His voice and asking Him to lead you where He wants you to go. If it is still unclear, look at the desires that are in your heart, and if they line up with God's Word and what you believe would please Him, I encourage you to walk in that direction. As I mentioned earlier, if you keep your heart humble and your ear listening for His voice, He will redirect you if you ever step off course. I believe as you step out in faith with God, you are going to be amazed at His goodness. I am still astounded that He chose to use my life to plant DC Metro Church, and I believe as you continue to surrender to Him, He wants to do something through your life that is even better than you can imagine.

My Personal Testimony

At the beginning of this book I shared with you the story of miraculously being healed of cancer when I was a teenager. This year marks twenty-five years of being cancer free! I hope that my testimony here encourages you to always seek God for any area of your life that needs healing or for anyone you love who needs healing. I fully believe that God is a God who still heals today, and I pray that my testimony will be your catalyst to continue to contend for full healing and wholeness in every area of life.

I share all of this to encourage you to pray for a breakthrough in whatever ailment, illness, or disease in your body or of someone you love. I am often asked why God does not heal in every situation, and while I cannot fully answer that question, I can tell you that those who choose to believe and pray for healing see breakthroughs at a much higher rate than those who don't. We are wise to choose to focus on what God is doing rather than focusing on what He is not doing. God is a God of hope, and you never know when your breakthrough could come, so I encourage you to keep seeking Him and to keep your heart alive to Him.

I have also seen incredible breakthroughs in my marriage and family. Although Taryn and I have been in love since we first started dating seventeen years ago, we have walked through some challenging seasons in our marriage and in our calling. The pressure of leading a growing church and family is real, and we were not immune to the weight of these struggles. Taryn received a prophetic word years before we were married that although she had grown up in a broken home, she would have a happy marriage and a happy family life. We named our home the Happy Nest as a prophetic declaration of the Word that had been given to her years earlier. We have stood upon this Word as we both worked hard to have a happy, healthy marriage and to raise our kids to have an authentic love for Jesus in a home where they can grow into who God is calling them to be.

Taryn threw me a surprise birthday party for my fortieth birthday. During the party, I was reflecting on God's goodness in our lives. I am encouraged to share with you that our marriage is as strong as it has ever been, and I am more in love with my wife than I was when she walked down the aisle to me thirteen years ago. Our three boys, Isaac, Josiah, and Asher, are full of energy and life, and Karis is our little princess. They have each brought us indescribable joy, as they, along with Taryn, are the best presents Jesus has ever given me. I am excited to see what God has for us as a family as we continue the incredible adventure of following His voice.

Is there a relationship in your life you are praying for? Maybe you are single and wondering if you are ever going to meet the right person. Perhaps you are in a difficult season in your marriage or one of your children is walking through a significant struggle. Maybe there is relational discord with someone you love and you do not know how to reconcile the relationship. Whatever the relational challenge you are experiencing, know that God wants to walk through the challenge with you. I encourage you to be one who chooses hope in each of these situations and believes these relationships can be restored.

This book contains testimonies about what happened when Taryn and I surrendered our lives to the Lord. The testimonies are of different ways God has spoken to me, Taryn, and others about our personal decisions and about the greater vision that He had for us and our church. You may not be called to do the same things I have done, but be assured God has a purpose for your life. Your sphere of influence may be different from mine, but God can do incredible things through your surrendered life as you continue to say yes to the adventure of being led by the Lord's voice!

As you position yourself to hear from Him, preparing to enter into the 40-Day Challenge, remember to communicate your results as you hear God's voice and experience Him moving in your life. I hope the results I've experienced have been an encouragement to you. God wants to use you to encourage someone else and invite them on a similar journey to know Him more!

PART THREE

THE EXPERIMENT—
A 40-DAY GUIDE
TO HEARING
GOD'S VOICE

In part one, I said that this book was written to help believers discover and apply specific knowledge to the practical dilemma of wanting to hear clearly from Him so that we can experience more depth in our relationship with Him. Throughout this book, I have explored ways you can position yourself to encounter the supernatural voice and leadings of God, and make contact with Him.

You started by asking God a question(or questions), and creating space and time in your life to hear from Him (Step One of the scientific method: Ask a Question). You learned about the still, small voice of God and of some of the different ways He will communicate with you.

You learned how to do background research, taking your question(s) and researching what the Word of God says about the topic (Step Two of the scientific method: Do Background Research). You are now familiar with the SOAP method of Bible study and the GOD SPA.

As you listen for His still, small voice and research the Word of God, you should discover a hypothesis of what you believe God is speaking to you (Step Three of the scientific method: Construct a Hypothesis). Next, you share what you believe God is speaking to you with trusted friends or counselors—testing to see if they confirm what you are hearing (Step Four of the scientific method: Test Your Hypothesis).

After this, you analyze what you have heard through His voice, His Word, and His counsel through others and see if your conclusion is confirmed by His peace (Step Five of the scientific method: Analyze Your Data and Draw a Conclusion). Finally, you tell others what you have learned through this process and what God has done in your life (Step Six of the scientific process: Communicate Your Results).

I have shared different ways that God speaks and how to recognize His voice, but the real purpose of this book is for you to hear God for yourself.

The Experiment

I challenge you to commit to the experiment I mentioned in the beginning of the book—a forty-day challenge designed to help you hear God and grow closer to Him. To that end I have created a guide that contains a forty-day devotional to help you implement the practices in this book and position yourself to hear from God.

The experiment's challenge is for you to practically apply what you have learned by spending thirty minutes each day in prayer and Bible study for the next forty days. I believe that God will meet you as you step out to seek Him. The promise of His guidance is stated in Psalm 32:8, "I will instruct you and teach you in the way you should go. I will guide you with my eye"[1] NKJV. There is no more important skill to gain than learning to recognize and follow His voice.

Before you jump into the actual devotional, I want to share some practical instructions on how to have a devo time. Whenever I am coaching anyone on how to hear from God, I encourage them to focus on five things, which I'll explain. I have yet to have someone come back to me later and say that they have not experienced a significant increase in being able to hear and discern His voice in their lives. At the end of the instructions is a short commitment for you to read and sign, acknowledging your desire to commit to the forty-day experiment.

Step One: Pick a time and a place to meet with God.

Before Taryn and I moved to Washington, D.C., to plant the church, I had been drawn to this area for many years because I knew it was a city of influence. If you can influence the D.C. area for Christ, you can influence the nation, and ultimately you will influence the world. Movers and shakers are attracted to D.C., and the people here tend to have an obsession with schedules and appointments. On more than one occasion I have heard someone say something to the effect of, "I have an opening three weeks from now for thirty minutes. Sorry, everything else is booked solid."

I have heard these same people confess that they struggle to find time to meet with God. My thought in pastoring them has been simple: How is it that we prioritize meetings with people we don't even like and neglect to meet with the God we love? I don't say this in a critical way but rather as a wakeup call and a reminder that we prioritize what we value. I challenge you to pull out your iPhone or your Day-Timer right now and literally schedule daily time with God.

This sounds simple, but it is all too easy to let the appointment slip if you do not tenaciously guard it. In my earlier years I was more sporadic in my devo times, but I found that missed appointments with God led to disappointments in life. How can I expect to find the abundant life He offers if I am not seeking Him each day to guide me into His fullness?

THE TIME:

I recommend that you choose the time when you are at your very best. I believe that God always gives us His very best, so I want to respond in suit by spending time with Him when I am most alert and ready to receive. Some people like getting up early, like 5 a.m.—that's great for them, but I am not at my best that early. I have found that God does not speak to me at that hour because . . . well, I am asleep (He can speak to me in my dreams if He wants to say anything to me before the sun rises). God is happy to meet with you any time of day, so what time works for you?

THE PLACE:

Next, find a place for you and God to meet. I recommend going somewhere you love. When I take Taryn out on a date, I do not choose a fast-food place because I want us to be somewhere we both love and enjoy. My organic, gluten-free-loving wife's love language is most certainly not some greasy french fries or being in an environment with screaming kids and dirty booths. Instead, I try to choose a healthy restaurant that has an atmosphere where we are able to connect with each other.

In a similar way, I recommend choosing a place for your time with God that you are excited to go to and a place that is conducive to connecting with Him. When I lived in my previous house, I would walk the neighborhood streets and pray. I am sure my neighbors wondered, *Who is this guy who paces the streets late at night in dark clothing talking to himself?*

When we moved to our new house, I decided that I didn't want to scare my neighbors or make them think I am any crazier than they probably already think I am, so I chose a new prayer strategy. Now I meet with God every day in my basement or in a special chair on my back porch overlooking the water, rolling hills, and the beautiful country landscape. It reminds me of where I grew up as a boy in Louisiana and helps me disconnect from the fast pace of the city so I can hear from Him.

If you are not able to be out in nature, I recommend preparing a place that you can make sacred. It could be a chair in a quiet room. It could even be your bed (if you can resist the temptation of dozing off). The most important part of choosing a place is that when you are there for your appointment with God, you can be fully present. Whenever I sit in my chair, I don't look at my phone or answer emails. It is time solely focused on Him and what He has to say. It is my best and my favorite meeting of the day.

I believe that God loves to come to places that are especially prepared for Him. It is our way to honor Him and demonstrate how excited we are for Him to come. In Exodus, the Lord tells Moses to tell the people to prepare for His coming. Exodus 19:10–11 says, "Go to the people and consecrate them today and tomorrow. Have them wash their clothes and be ready by the third day, because on that day the Lord will come down on Mount Sinai in the sight of all the people."

On the third morning there was thunder, lightning, and a thick cloud over the mountain. God showed up in a spectacular way in response to His people's preparation to hear from Him. There was a trumpet blast before Moses spoke. Then God answered. I don't know about you, but my devo times are not usually quite this dramatic. But I have found that when I prepare a time and a place to meet with Him, He shows up.

There is a classic eighties flick that I love called *Field of Dreams*. The movie is about an Iowa farmer who hears a voice telling him, "If you build it, he will come." Although in the movie it is referring to building a baseball field for the Chicago Black Sox, I have found this principle to be true in my relationship with God. If you prepare a place for Him and build in a time to be with Him, He will show up. If you build it, He will come!

Once you have picked a time and a place, what do you do next?

Step Two: *Be still and worship.*

Psalm 46:10 says to "be still and know that I am God." Honestly, I am not always good at being still. I would definitely rather be moving, preferably at a very high speed. Fortunately, the Hebrew word for the phrase "be still" is *raphah,* which is not necessarily a literal stillness but more of a stillness of the soul. Psalm 46:10 can be translated as: "Stop striving and know that I am God." The context of this passage was at a time when Israel was being threatened by other nations. In the midst of these threats, the Israelites could trust in the covenant that God made with them and know that He would be their very present help, refuge, and strength (see Psalm 46:1).

There is something about being still before God that reminds us we are not in charge—He is. Once we are still before Him, we can enter into true worship. I have found that when I worship, everything shifts. If my perspective was off, I see rightly once again. I am reminded of the bigness of God and of how much He loves me and how much I love Him. I am also reminded again of how much I need Him and how trustworthy He is.

I have not always begun my devo times with worship, but I highly recommend taking some time to worship before you jump into reading the Word. Worship helps you release burdens you are carrying and shifts your perspective so you see rightly again. Sometimes I will put a song on repeat so that the words wash over me again and again. Our hearts become more surrendered and tenderized in His presence. We were made to worship.

It is during my time of being still and worshipping that I often bring my questions and requests to God (Step One of the scientific method). As I am still before Him and aware of His presence, my heart opens to Him—I share with Him what is in my heart.

Step Three: **Read and pray.**

God has written down His opinions and wisdom regarding the most common problems we face, so I recommend spending time looking at what He says in His Word—Step Two of the scientific method. There is an integral partnership between the Word and the Spirit when it comes to God speaking. As you open your Bible and read, you are hearing what God has already spoken and asking the Holy Spirit to make those words come alive so you can discern what God is speaking to you.

In chapter 2, I gave you some basic Bible study tools that have worked in my personal devos. We have included a daily passage from the Bible for each of your forty days in the 40-Day Challenge. After you complete the experiment, we recommend you try one of the following options:

1. **A topical study:** Take one of the questions that you have been asking God or a question that He has already answered. Look for what the Bible has to say around that question or issue. For example: if you are asking God's direction on marriage, search out in a concordance or in an online search (on websites such as BibleGateway.com) those passages in the Bible that deal with marriage. If you are asking Him for wisdom on some decisions you have to make, what does the Bible say about wisdom? Your study will often either confirm something He has already spoken or direct you to your question's answer.

2. *A book or character study:* Choose a book of the Bible to study, or choose a person from the Bible to study.

Since the experiment is to spend thirty minutes a day with God, I recommend you start by spending ten to fifteen of those minutes in study after you worship. As you get into the Word, that time will likely increase. Sometimes I study for hours, looking up Greek and Hebrew words and cross-referencing passages in the Bible. Other times I spend just a few minutes reading a few verses.

Sometimes I feel as though God is speaking directly to me through His Word, and I understand exactly what He is asking me to do next through something I read. Other times, when I read, God feels abstract and I struggle to understand how the passage has any correlation to my life whatsoever. This is very normal. Keep reading. As you continue to read with your ears and heart open, He will speak to you.

I believe that reading the Bible is meant to be an interactive experience—God wants you to dialogue with Him as you are reading, so I recommend praying as you are reading and again after you read. I often ask Him what He means in certain passages or how I can apply certain words of wisdom that I read to my current situations. The Word of God was never meant to be mere moral instructions but a launchpad into an interaction with God, so if you are not talking to God as you read, you are missing the point.

After you finish reading, take a few minutes to respond in prayer to what you read. Pray about whatever is on your heart—those questions from Step One of the scientific method. Many people lose traction in prayer because they think they need to be praying about major world issues. If those big topics are on your heart, go for it, but if you are distracted by the fight you just had with your significant other or your friend, pray about that first. Maybe you are struggling with feeling overwhelmed by all your responsibilities at work or home and the weight you have gained recently from stress eating or with feeling like you can't make traction in your finances. Pray about what is in your heart. God desires authenticity more than manufactured piety.

Often when I am trying to pray for more than a minute or two, my mind starts to wander. When that happens, I have found it extremely helpful to write down my prayers, or sometimes I pray out loud as I pace back and forth in my basement. This brings us to the next step in how we can practically position ourselves to hear the supernatural voice of God.

Step Four: Listen and write.

I recently heard that the above average person only listens for approximately seventeen seconds before diverting the conversation back to themselves. It seems that we are just naturally egocentric unless we intentionally guard against it. To illustrate this point, when you see a group picture, who is the first person you look at? What criteria do you use to determine if you like the picture—how your friend looks or whether the angle is flattering for the person next to you? I didn't think so.

In our relationship with God and with others, most of us struggle with being good listeners, but we will miss many important promptings from God if we do not take the time to listen for the still, small voice of God.[2] Do you pause to listen to God, or do you spend most of your time rattling off prayer requests?

Prayer is meant to be a two-way conversation. I know some people get frustrated when they hear pastors and teachers say that because they struggle to hear from God when they stop to listen, so they just keep talking.

This wrestling can come from many places, and it is important to discern its root so that you can address it. It could be from a place of doubt—some people don't believe He is really going to speak to them or trust that they can discern His voice. Other times it can come from wrong teaching—some people today have been taught in Christian churches that He does not speak to us personally, so they don't even try. It can also come from fear—some people have stopped trying to listen to what He is saying because they are fearful of what He might ask them to do. It could even be busyness—some of us don't stop and listen simply because we are always on the run.

If you struggle to listen, what is the root motive? Confess this to God and ask Him to help you take time to listen, believing that He wants to talk with you and that whatever He asks is for your ultimate good.

TWO-WAY JOURNALING:

As I shared in chapter 2, the single most revolutionary step I have taken in the past several years to dramatically increase both the amount of time I spend listening and the frequency I hear from God is something I call two-way journaling. To refresh your memory, go back and review that section in chapter 2.

You first write God an honest and authentic letter, thank Him for who He is, release any burdens, ask Him questions, lift up your requests, or invite Him to speak into your life situations or problems. Then write yourself a letter from God. He may encourage you, or bring scriptures to your mind that deal with your struggles or questions. When you finish journaling, submit everything back to God and ask Him to make clear or redirect you in what you heard. Test everything with the same filters you do any time you are attempting to hear from God.

You will have an opportunity to try two-way journaling as a part of your devotional time in the 40-Day Challenge. If this is a new exercise for you, I believe you will enjoy this focused way of processing with the Lord and hearing what He says as you write!

Step Five: *Share and obey.*

With whom can you share what God spoke to you? If it is direction you received, it is wise to share this with the godly counsel in your life. As I shared in chapter 3, I am committed to always having close, godly counsel and have given them permission to speak into my life and hold me accountable.

After you have shared with godly counsel in your life in order to seek their direction and accountability, ask God if there is anyone else He wants you to tell about what He has done or how He has met you. If it is a revelation or insight He has showed you, think about who could benefit from hearing what God has been teaching you. Is there someone in your life going through something similar that might be encouraged by your story or what God has spoken to you?

I encourage you to be ready to tell whomever God brings in your path, even if it is a stranger you meet on an airplane or someone who is a casual acquaintance. Dr. Umidi, one of DC Metro's Overseers, talks about how God loves to use us as "UPS men" because He has special-delivery packages for divine appointments in our lives. This special-delivery package could be you telling the story of something God just walked you through or a revelation God shared with you in your devo time. As you walk in step with the Holy Spirit, He will highlight exactly who and what to share. Will you step out in obedience?

As a final step in the process, spend some time asking God if there are any additional steps of obedience or action steps He would like you to take. Or if there is something He has already showed you to do, commit to walking that out and commit to the time frame you will need to complete it. Colossians 3:15 instructs us to let God's peace lead us. This is a helpful reminder when we feel challenged to obey or step out because His peace is a tangible reminder of His presence with us.

As you begin the 40-Day Challenge, note that I structured it after the devo format above that I personally follow. For me, the scientific method steps that I talked about in the earlier chapters fit well into the devo format.

The Commitment

I included this simple commitment between you and God, because I believe your commitment to the experiment will radically change your life. Read it, decide if you are ready to take the plunge, sign, and date.

My Commitment to God

I have read and understand the basic steps for hearing the voice of God introduced in *Hearing from God*. I am excited about the opportunity to develop my relationship with God, learning how to spend time in His presence and Word, and growing in my ability to hear from Him. I consider it an honor that God desires to communicate with me and an adventure to learn how to make contact with Him!

I recognize that my desire to know him needs an investment of my time and discipline. Therefore, for the next forty days, I commit to the following:

1. I will purposely position myself to hear from God, scheduling a time and place to daily meet with Him.

2. I will follow the suggested devo format Pastor David introduced: spending time in stillness and worship, reading the Word of God, praying, and two-way journaling.

3. I will find a trusted friend or friends to serve as godly counsel and share what I am learning and believe God is speaking to me.

4. Finally, I will step out in obedience and do whatever He calls me to do, including sharing with others what God is doing in my life.

I recognize that my commitment for the next forty days is the start of a new dimension in my relationship with God, and the principles that I put into practice during this time will lay the foundation for a lifelong experience of making contact with God!

_____   _____
My Signature   Date

PART FOUR

The 40-Day Challenge

The 40-Day Challenge

Now that you have read about how to position yourself to hear from God through the steps that correlate to the scientific method, it is your turn! The whole purpose of the scientific method is to prove or disprove a hypothesis. My hypothesis is not just that God speaks but that God wants to speak to you personally. The only way to find out if this is true is to perform the experiment on yourself.

You have read about my stories of success, my adventures, and my supernatural breakthroughs that came from following His voice. I now challenge you to come on this forty-day journey with God I have called "The Experiment." I believe you will love this process and I am praying that it will become a lifestyle of hearing from God. I am excited for you to experience your own stories of success, adventures with God, and supernatural breakthroughs in your life. I believe you will have success in hearing from God, adventures in obeying what He says, and supernatural breakthroughs in whatever area of spiritual growth you are seeking Him.

On page 119, you will find a sample entry of someone named Susan on the first day of her forty-day journey. As you read her entry, you will notice her realness and transparency. I believe it is absolutely critical that you are completely authentic with God (remember, yours will not be published in a book!).

Here are a few tips I have found to be helpful in each step:

1. **Pick a Time and a Place:** Pick a time where you are at your best and a place where you will not be distracted.

2. **Be Still and Worship:** Worship until you sense God is in the room because He is. I encourage you to talk with God as though He is right in front of you. There is a big difference between knowing that He is an ever-present help and believing that He is an ever-present help for you.

3. **Read and Pray:** As you go through the experiment, I have selected scriptures that I believe will help you hear from God with ease. Remember that this is something His voice has said, is saying, and will be saying for all of eternity. You can keep an open notebook by you to jot down anything that comes to mind—such as your to-do list—while you are praying so you won't get sidetracked.

4. **Listen and Write:** Take a moment to listen for anything God may be saying after you pray. When you begin to write your letter to God, write about whatever is on your mind and, remember, you can be raw and real—don't hold back. After you have finished writing to God, ask Him what He wants to say to you. When you write the letter to yourself from God, don't worry about questioning whether each word is from God because you can test it later through Scripture and godly counsel. Focus on what you believe God is saying to you and write freely.

5. **Share and Obey:** If you have received specific direction from God, focus on sharing and processing it with your SAFE people. Then, by obeying God, you will experience adventures, success, and supernatural breakthroughs that bring victory by following where He leads!

Welcome to what I believe could be one of the best seasons of your life as you follow Him. I am praying for you as you embark on this incredible journey!

SAMPLE DEVO PAGE

Here is a sample devo page from a woman named Susan. It will give you an idea of what a completed devo time looks like. Note, Susan didn't fill out all the points in GOD SPA. She only responded to those that were relevant to what God was dealing with her on that specific day.

Sample Day
Romans 12:1–10

1. **Time and Place**—When and where did you meet with God?

7:30–8:00 a.m. in the lounge chair in the guest bedroom.

2. **Be Still and Worship** (5–10 minutes)—Turn on worship music and ask God to help you connect to Him. Start by telling Him how wonderful He is and thanking Him for ways He's blessed your life. Ask if there is any burden you need to release to Him. After you are finished, write down any impressions, thoughts, or themes you felt during your time of worship.

Quickly recognized that I have been feeling heavy about the lack of work the past couple weeks. Told Him I was sorry for not trusting Him, and asked Him to take the burden I've been carrying. I was reminded that He is always faithful, even when I can't see what He is doing.

3. **Read and Pray** (10–15 minutes)—Read the following passage and use the SOAP method and the GOD SPA questions:

> "Therefore, I urge you, brothers and sisters, in view of God's mercy, to offer your bodies as a living sacrifice, holy and pleasing to God—this is your true and proper worship. Do not conform to the pattern of this world, but be transformed by the renewing of your mind. Then you will be able to test and ap-

prove what God's will is—his good, pleasing and perfect will. For by the grace given me I say to every one of you: Do not think of yourself more highly than you ought, but rather think of yourself with sober judgment, in accordance with the faith God has distributed to each of you. For just as each of us has one body with many members, and these members do not all have the same function, so in Christ we, though many, form one body, and each member belongs to all the others. We have different gifts, according to the grace given to each of us. If your gift is prophesying, then prophesy in accordance with your faith; if it is serving, then serve; if it is teaching, then teach; if it is to encourage, then give encouragement; if it is giving, then give generously; if it is to lead, do it diligently; if it is to show mercy, do it cheerfully. Love must be sincere. Hate what is evil; cling to what is good. Be devoted to one another in love. Honor one another above yourselves." (Romans 12:1–10)

Observation—What stands out to you in this passage?

That worship is not just what we do on Sunday at church! It is giving my whole life to God as a sacrifice. This is the kind of devotion that pleases God. Also, it seems that the idea of giving our bodies as a living sacrifice is explained in verse 2: not conforming to the world, getting a new mind, and figuring out what God's will is for me.

Application—How can you apply this passage to your life? (You may not have all of these answered for every passage, but it is helpful to ask the following questions.) Is there a/an:

Growth Area?

I need to work on the not conforming part, and renewing my mind. It kind of fits with my feeling heavy about no work.....Instead of trusting God with my whole life, I tend to try to take control when I don't think He has me covered. I get pushy, bossy, and manipulative and think negative thoughts about everything and everyone.

Obedience Needed?
Recommit my life to Him. I will ask Him to show me what His will is for my life concerning work-and needing to pay my bills! What do I need to do that I'm not doing?

Direction to Follow?

Sin to Confess?
Already did this!

Promise to Claim?
I can know God's will if I live my life as a living sacrifice to Him!

Accountability?
Getting rid of the negative and critical thinking about circumstances and people.

Prayer—Spend a minute in prayer asking God to help you apply these truths to your life.

4. **Write and Listen** (10–15 minutes)—Write a letter to God. This can be in response to what He was saying to you through Scripture, or you can write Him about anything that is on your mind.

Dear God,

Thanks for taking care of me, even when I don't see or understand what you are doing in my life. I belong to you, so keep on working on my character and my thoughts so that they will be pleasing to you. I do trust you in my head; help me trust you in my heart and experience.

The work situation has been difficult. And I've had a hard time not carrying the burden of my financial needs. I see the pile of bills each morning. The past couple weeks I haven't seen where the money to pay those bills is coming from. I'm sorry because I know that you see the bills, too, and probably have a great plan to meet my needs—if I only chill a little and let you take the burden. Show me what I need to do about work and the bills!

I'm not sure I'm totally comfortable with the image of being a sacrifice. I guess that means some desires and other things in my life have to die. More than any discomfort I might feel, I want to be pleasing to you, so here I am. Help me so I won't be pushed and molded into what the world wants me to be. Also, help me with my negative and critical thoughts. I'm going to work on that, but I sure need you to help keep me in check. I love you!

Susan

Listen for what God is saying to you. Write a letter to yourself from God with what you believe He is saying in response to you.

Dear Susan,

Your desire to know me and my purposes in your life makes me happy. I've promised to meet your physical needs, so relax and I will help you grow in your ability to trust. I do see what you need, and see it long before you are even aware. When you take control and worry, you lose sight of who I am and overlook the many ways I am at work in your situation. I will meet your needs when you have a job and are working hard, and I will meet your needs when you are unemployed and work is slow. Ultimately, I am your provider-depend on and trust me, instead of putting your trust in a biweekly paycheck. I love to show up for you and surprise you with my goodness. Get ready!

I will help you to grow in your relationship with me. I desire that you know me and my ways even more than you desire it. I see your desire to be pleasing to me, and that means so much to me. As you lay your life down as a living sacrifice, I will work in you to help you conform to my will and purposes for you. Trust me and obey me and see what I am able to do in your heart, mind, and your circumstances.

Love, your Father

5. **Share and Obey** (After devo is completed)—With whom can you share what God spoke to you? If it is direction you received, it is wise to share this with the godly counsel in your life, and if it is revelation or insight, think about who would be encouraged to hear what God has been teaching you and who can hold you accountable to what He spoke.

I want to tell Katie all about the trust issues that

I have been dealing with about no work, and that I am recommitting myself as that living sacrifice.

What steps of obedience or action steps are you going to take? Colossians 3:15 reminds us to let God's peace lead us when we feel challenged to obey or step out because His peace is a tangible reminder of His presence with us.

Talk to Katie. Continue to ask God what I need to be doing differently, until I get some specific direction.

DAILY DEVO PAGES

John 10:1-10

1. **Time and Place**—When and where did you meet with God?

....

....

....

2. **Be Still and Worship** (5–10 minutes)—Turn on worship music and ask God to help you connect to Him. Start by telling Him how wonderful He is and ask if there is any burden you need to release to Him. After you are finished, write down any impressions, thoughts, or themes you felt during your time of worship.

....

....

3. **Read and Pray** (10–15 minutes)—Read the following passage and use the SOAP method and the GOD SPA questions:

> "'Very truly I tell you Pharisees, anyone who does not enter the sheep pen by the gate, but climbs in by some other way, is a thief and a robber. The one who enters by the gate is the shepherd of the sheep. The gatekeeper opens the gate for him, and the sheep listen to his voice. He calls his own sheep by name and leads them out. When he has brought out all his own, he goes on ahead of them, and his sheep follow him because they know his voice. But they will never follow a stranger; in fact, they will run away from him because they do not recognize a stranger's voice.' Jesus used this figure of speech, but the Pharisees did not understand what he was telling them. Therefore Jesus said again, 'Very truly I tell you, I am the gate for the sheep. All who have come before me are thieves and robbers,

but the sheep have not listened to them. I am the gate; whoever enters through me will be saved. They will come in and go out, and find pasture. The thief comes only to steal and kill and destroy; I have come that they may have life, and have it to the full.'" (John 10:1–10)

Observation—What stands out to you in this passage?

....

....

....

Application—(You may not have all of these answered for every passage, but it is helpful to ask the following questions). Is there a/an:

Growth Area?

....

....

....

Obedience Needed?

....

....

....

Direction to Follow?

....

....

....

Sin to Confess?

....

....

....

Promise to Claim?

....

....

....

Accountability?

....

....

....

Prayer—Spend a minute in prayer asking God to help you apply these truths to your life.

4. **Write and Listen** (10–15 minutes)—Write a letter to God. This can be in response to what He was saying to you through Scripture or you can write Him about anything that is on your mind.

....

....

....

....

....

....

....

....

....

....

....

....

....

....

....

....

Listen for what God is saying to you. Write a letter to yourself from God with what you believe He is saying in response to you.

....
....
....
....
....
....
....
....
....
....
....
....
....
....
....
....
....

5. Share and Obey (After devo is completed)—With whom can you share what God spoke to you? If it is direction you received, it is wise to share this with the godly counsel in your life, and if it is revelation or insight, think about who would be encouraged to hear what God has been teaching you and who can hold you accountable to what He spoke.

....
....
....

What steps of obedience or action steps are you going to take?

....
....
....

Psalm 32:7–11

1. **Time and Place**—When and where did you meet with God?

....

....

....

2. **Be Still and Worship** (5–10 minutes)—Turn on worship music and ask God to help you connect to Him. Start by telling Him how wonderful He is and ask if there is any burden you need to release to Him. After you are finished, write down any impressions, thoughts, or themes you felt during your time of worship.

....

....

....

....

3. **Read and Pray** (10–15 minutes)—Read the following passage and use the SOAP method and the GOD SPA questions:

> "You are my hiding place; you will protect me from trouble and surround me with songs of deliverance. I will instruct you and teach you in the way you should go; I will counsel you with my loving eye on you. Do not be like the horse or the mule, which have no understanding but must be controlled by bit and bridle or they will not come to you. Many are the woes of the wicked, but the Lord's unfailing love surrounds the one who trusts in him. Rejoice in the Lord and be glad, you righteous; sing, all who are upright in heart!" (Psalm 32:7–11)

Observation—What stands out to you in this passage?

....
....
....
....

Application—How can you apply this passage to your life? (You may not have all of these answered for every passage, but it is helpful to ask the following questions.) Is there a/an:

Growth Area?

....
....
....

Obedience Needed?

....
....
....

Direction to Follow?

....
....
....

Sin to Confess?

....
....
....

Promise to Claim?

....
....
....

Accountability?

....

....

....

Prayer—Spend a minute in prayer asking God to help you apply these truths to your life.

4. **Write and Listen** (10–15 minutes)—Write a letter to God. This can be in response to what He was saying to you through Scripture, or you can write Him about anything that is on your mind.

....

....

....

....

....

....

....

....

....

....

....

....

....

....

....

....

....

....

....

....

....

....

Listen for what God is saying to you. Write a letter to yourself from God with what you believe He is saying in response to you.

....

....

....

....

....

....

....

....

....

....

....

....

....

....

....

....

5. **Share and Obey** (After devo is completed)—With whom can you share what God spoke to you? If it is direction you received, it is wise to share this with the godly counsel in your life, and if it is revelation or insight, think about who would be encouraged to hear what God has been teaching you and who can hold you accountable to what He spoke.

....

....

....

What steps of obedience or action steps are you going to take?

....

....

....

Ephesians 3:14–21

1. Time and Place—When and where did you meet with God?

....

....

....

2. Be Still and Worship (5–10 minutes)—Turn on worship music and ask God to help you connect to Him. Start by telling Him how wonderful He is and ask if there is any burden you need to release to Him. After you are finished, write down any impressions, thoughts, or themes you felt during your time of worship.

....

....

....

3. Read and Pray (10–15 minutes)—Read the following passage and use the SOAP method and the GOD SPA questions:

"For this reason I kneel before the Father, from whom every family in heaven and on earth derives its name. I pray that out of his glorious riches he may strengthen you with power through his Spirit in your inner being, so that Christ may dwell in your hearts through faith. And I pray that you, being rooted and established in love, may have power, together with all the Lord's holy people, to grasp how wide and long and high and deep is the love of Christ, and to know this love that surpasses knowledge—that you may be filled to the measure of all the fullness of God. Now to Him who is able to do immeasurably more than all we ask or imagine, according to His power that is at work within us, to Him be glory in the church and in Christ

Jesus throughout all generations, for ever and ever! Amen."
(Ephesians 3:14–21)

Observation—What stands out to you in this passage?

....

....

....

Application—How can you apply this passage to your life? (You may not have all of these answered for every passage, but it is helpful to ask the following questions.) Is there a/an:

Growth Area?

....

....

....

Obedience Needed?

....

....

Direction to Follow?

....

....

....

Sin to Confess?

....

....

....

Promise to Claim?

....

....

Accountability?

....

....

....

Prayer—Spend a minute in prayer asking God to help you apply these truths to your life.

4. **Write and Listen** (10–15 minutes)—Write a letter to God. This can be in response to what He was saying to you through Scripture, or you can write Him about anything that is on your mind.

....

....

....

....

....

....

....

....

....

....

....

....

....

....

....

....

....

....

....

....

Listen for what God is saying to you. Write a letter to yourself from God with what you believe He is saying in response to you.

....

....

....

....

....

....

....

....

....

....

....

....

....

....

....

....

5. **Share and Obey** (After devo is completed)—With whom can you share what God spoke to you? If it is direction you received, it is wise to share this with the godly counsel in your life, and if it is revelation or insight, think about who would be encouraged to hear what God has been teaching you and who can hold you accountable to what He spoke.

....

....

....

What steps of obedience or action steps are you going to take?

....

....

....

John 6:5–15

1. **Time and Place**—When and where did you meet with God?

....

....

....

2. **Be Still and Worship** (5–10 minutes)—Turn on worship music and ask God to help you connect to Him. Start by telling Him how wonderful He is and ask if there is any burden you need to release to Him. After you are finished, write down any impressions, thoughts, or themes you felt during your time of worship.

....

....

....

3. **Read and Pray** (10–15 minutes)—Read the following passage and use the SOAP method and the GOD SPA questions:

> "When Jesus looked up and saw a great crowd coming toward him, he said to Philip, 'Where shall we buy bread for these people to eat?' He asked this only to test him, for he already had in mind what he was going to do. Philip answered him, 'It would take more than half a year's wages to buy enough bread for each one to have a bite!' Another of his disciples, Andrew, Simon Peter's brother, spoke up, 'Here is a boy with five small barley loaves and two small fish, but how far will they go among so many?' Jesus said, 'Have the people sit down.' There was plenty of grass in that place, and they sat down (about five thousand men were there). Jesus then took the loaves, gave thanks, and distributed to those who were seated as much as they wanted.

He did the same with the fish. When they had all had enough
to eat, He said to His disciples, 'Gather the pieces that are left
over. Let nothing be wasted.' So they gathered them and filled
twelve baskets with the pieces of the five barley loaves left over
by those who had eaten. After the people saw the sign Jesus
performed, they began to say, 'Surely this is the Prophet who is
to come into the world.' Jesus, knowing that they intended to
come and make Him king by force, withdrew again to a mountain by Himself." (John 6:5–15)

Observation—What stands out to you in this passage?

....

....

....

....

Application—How can you apply this passage to your life? (You may not
have all of these answered for every passage, but it is helpful to ask the
following questions.) Is there a/an:

Growth Area?

....

....

....

Obedience Needed?

....

....

....

Direction to Follow?

....

....

....

Sin to Confess?

....

....

....

Promise to Claim?

....

....

....

Accountability?

....

....

....

Prayer—Spend a minute in prayer asking God to help you apply these truths to your life.

4. **Write and Listen** (10–15 minutes)—Write a letter to God. This can be in response to what He was saying to you through Scripture, or you can write Him about anything that is on your mind.

....

....

....

....

....

....

....

....

....

....

....

....

Listen for what God is saying to you. Write a letter to yourself from God with what you believe He is saying in response to you.

....
....
....
....
....
....
....
....
....
....
....
....
....
....
....
....

5. **Share and Obey** (After devo is completed)—With whom can you share what God spoke to you? If it is direction you received, it is wise to share this with the godly counsel in your life, and if it is revelation or insight, think about who would be encouraged to hear what God has been teaching you and who can hold you accountable to what He spoke.

....
....
....
....

What steps of obedience or action steps are you going to take?

....
....
....

Psalm 51:10–17

1. **Time and Place**—When and where did you meet with God?

....

....

....

2. **Be Still and Worship** (5–10 minutes)—Turn on worship music and ask God to help you connect to Him. Start by telling Him how wonderful He is and ask if there is any burden you need to release to Him. After you are finished, write down any impressions, thoughts, or themes you felt during your time of worship.

....

....

....

3. **Read and Pray** (10–15 minutes)—Read the following passage and use the SOAP method and the GOD SPA questions:

> "Create in me a pure heart, O God, and renew a steadfast spirit within me. Do not cast me from your presence or take your Holy Spirit from me. Restore to me the joy of your salvation and grant me a willing spirit, to sustain me. Then I will teach transgressors your ways, so that sinners will turn back to you. Deliver me from the guilt of bloodshed, O God, you who are God my Savior, and my tongue will sing of your righteousness. Open my lips, Lord, and my mouth will declare your praise. You do not delight in sacrifice, or I would bring it; you do not take pleasure in burnt offerings. My sacrifice, O God, is a broken spirit; a broken and contrite heart, you, God, will not despise." (Psalm 51:10–17)

Observation—What stands out to you in this passage?

....

....

....

....

Application—How can you apply this passage to your life? (You may not have all of these answered for every passage, but it is helpful to ask the following questions.) Is there a/an:

Growth Area?

....

....

....

Obedience Needed?

....

....

....

Direction to Follow?

....

....

....

Sin to Confess?

....

....

....

Promise to Claim?

....

....

....

Accountability?

....

....

....

Prayer—Spend a minute in prayer asking God to help you apply these truths to your life.

4. **Write and Listen** (10–15 minutes)—Write a letter to God. This can be in response to what He was saying to you through Scripture, or you can write Him about anything that is on your mind.

....

....

....

....

....

....

....

....

....

....

....

....

....

....

....

....

....

....

....

....

....

....

....

....

Listen for what God is saying to you. Write a letter to yourself from God with what you believe He is saying in response to you.

....
....
....
....
....
....
....
....
....
....
....
....
....
....
....

5. **Share and Obey** (After devo is completed)—With whom can you share what God spoke to you? If it is direction you received, it is wise to share this with the godly counsel in your life, and if it is revelation or insight, think about who would be encouraged to hear what God has been teaching you and who can hold you accountable to what He spoke.

....
....
....

What steps of obedience or action steps are you going to take?

....
....
....

Philippians 2:1-11

1. **Time and Place**—When and where did you meet with God?

....

....

....

2. **Be Still and Worship** (5–10 minutes)—Turn on worship music and ask God to help you connect to Him. Start by telling Him how wonderful He is and ask if there is any burden you need to release to Him. After you are finished, write down any impressions, thoughts, or themes you felt during your time of worship.

....

....

....

3. **Read and Pray** (10–15 minutes)—Read the following passage and use the SOAP method and the GOD SPA questions:

> "Therefore if you have any encouragement from being united with Christ, if any comfort from his love, if any common sharing in the Spirit, if any tenderness and compassion, then make my joy complete by being like-minded, having the same love, being one in spirit and of one mind. Do nothing out of self-ish ambition or vain conceit. Rather, in humility value others above yourselves, not looking to your own interests but each of you to the interests of the others. In your relationships with one another, have the same mindset as Christ Jesus: Who, being in very nature God, did not consider equality with God something to be used to his own advantage; rather, he made himself nothing by taking the very nature of a servant, being

made in human likeness. And being found in appearance as a man, He humbled Himself by becoming obedient to death—even death on a cross! Therefore God exalted him to the highest place and gave him the name that is above every name, that at the name of Jesus every knee should bow, in heaven and on earth and under the earth, and every tongue acknowledge that Jesus Christ is Lord, to the glory of God the Father." (Philippians 2:1–11)

Observation—What stands out to you in this passage?

....

....

....

....

....

Application—How can you apply this passage to your life? (You may not have all of these answered for every passage, but it is helpful to ask the following questions.) Is there a/an:

Growth Area?

....

....

....

Obedience Needed?

....

....

....

Direction to Follow?

....

....

....

Sin to Confess?

....

....

....

Promise to Claim?

....

....

....

Accountability?

....

....

....

Prayer—Spend a minute in prayer asking God to help you apply these truths to your life.

4. **Write and Listen** (10–15 minutes)—Write a letter to God. This can be in response to what He was saying to you through Scripture, or you can write Him about anything that is on your mind.

....

....

....

....

....

....

....

....

....

....

....

Listen for what God is saying to you. Write a letter to yourself from God
with what you believe He is saying in response to you.

....

....

....

....

....

....

....

....

....

....

....

....

....

....

....

....

5. **Share and Obey** (After devo is completed)—With whom can you
share what God spoke to you? If it is direction you received, it is wise to
share this with the godly counsel in your life, and if it is revelation or insight, think about who would be encouraged to hear what God has been
teaching you and who can hold you accountable to what He spoke.

....

....

....

What steps of obedience or action steps are you going to take?

....

....

....

Joshua 1:1-9

1. Time and Place—When and where did you meet with God?

....

....

....

2. Be Still and Worship (5–10 minutes)—Turn on worship music and ask God to help you connect to Him. Start by telling Him how wonderful He is and ask if there is any burden you need to release to Him. After you are finished, write down any impressions, thoughts, or themes you felt during your time of worship.

....

....

....

3. Read and Pray (10–15 minutes)—Read the following passage and use the SOAP method and the GOD SPA questions:

"After the death of Moses the servant of the Lord, the Lord said to Joshua son of Nun, Moses' aide: 'Moses my servant is dead. Now then, you and all these people, get ready to cross the Jordan River into the land I am about to give to them—to the Israelites. I will give you every place where you set your foot, as I promised Moses. Your territory will extend from the desert to Lebanon, and from the great river, the Euphrates—all the Hittite country—to the Mediterranean Sea in the west. No one will be able to stand against you all the days of your life. As I was with Moses, so I will be with you; I will never leave you nor forsake you. Be strong and courageous, because you will lead these people to inherit the land I swore to their ancestors to give them. Be strong and very courageous. Be careful to obey all the law my servant Moses gave you; do not turn from it to the right or to the left, that you may be successful wherever you go. Keep this Book of the Law always on your lips; meditate on it day and night, so that you may be careful to do everything written in it. Then you will be prosperous and successful. Have I not commanded you? Be strong and courageous. Do not be afraid; do not be discouraged, for the Lord your God will be with you wherever you go.'" (Joshua 1:1–9)

Observation—What stands out to you in this passage?

....
....
....
....

Application—How can you apply this passage to your life? (You may not have all of these answered for every passage, but it is helpful to ask the following questions.) Is there a/an:

Growth Area?

....
....
....

Obedience Needed?

....
....
....

Direction to Follow?

....
....
....

Sin to Confess?

....

....

....

Promise to Claim?

....

....

....

Accountability?

....

....

....

Prayer—Spend a minute in prayer asking God to help you apply these truths to your life.

4. **Write and Listen** (10–15 minutes)—Write a letter to God. This can be in response to what He was saying to you through Scripture, or you can write Him about anything that is on your mind.

....

....

....

....

....

....

....

....

....

....

....

....

Listen for what God is saying to you. Write a letter to yourself from God with what you believe He is saying in response to you.

....
....
....
....
....
....
....
....
....
....
....
....
....
....
....
....

5. **Share and Obey** (After devo is completed)—With whom can you share what God spoke to you? If it is direction you received, it is wise to share this with the godly counsel in your life, and if it is revelation or insight, think about who would be encouraged to hear what God has been teaching you and who can hold you accountable to what He spoke.

....
....
....

What steps of obedience or action steps are you going to take?

....
....
....

Exodus 14:13–22

1. Time and Place—When and where did you meet with God?

....

....

....

2. Be Still and Worship (5–10 minutes)—Turn on worship music and ask God to help you connect to Him. Start by telling Him how wonderful He is and ask if there is any burden you need to release to Him. After you are finished, write down any impressions, thoughts, or themes you felt during your time of worship.

....

....

....

3. Read and Pray (10–15 minutes)—Read the following passage and use the SOAP method and the GOD SPA questions:

> "Moses answered the people, 'Do not be afraid. Stand firm and you will see the deliverance the Lord will bring you today. The Egyptians you see today you will never see again. The Lord will fight for you; you need only to be still.' Then the Lord said to Moses, 'Why are you crying out to me? Tell the Israelites to move on. Raise your staff and stretch out your hand over the sea to divide the water so that the Israelites can go through the sea on dry ground. I will harden the hearts of the Egyptians so that they will go in after them. And I will gain glory through Pharaoh and all his army, through his chariots and his horsemen. The Egyptians will know that I am the Lord when I gain glory through Pharaoh, his chariots and his horsemen.' Then

the angel of God, who had been traveling in front of Israel's army, withdrew and went behind them. The pillar of cloud also moved from in front and stood behind them, coming between the armies of Egypt and Israel. Throughout the night the cloud brought darkness to the one side and light to the other side; so neither went near the other all night long. Then Moses stretched out his hand over the sea, and all that night the Lord drove the sea back with a strong east wind and turned it into dry land. The waters were divided, and the Israelites went through the sea on dry ground, with a wall of water on their right and on their left." (Exodus 14:13–22)

Observation—What stands out to you in this passage?

....

....

....

Application—How can you apply this passage to your life? (You may not have all of these answered for every passage, but it is helpful to ask the following questions.) Is there a/an:

Growth Area?

....

....

....

Obedience Needed?

....

....

....

Direction to Follow?

....

....

Sin to Confess?

....
....
....

Promise to Claim?

....
....
....

Accountability?

....
....
....

Prayer—Spend a minute in prayer asking God to help you apply these truths to your life.

4. **Write and Listen** (10–15 minutes)—Write a letter to God. This can be in response to what He was saying to you through Scripture, or you can write Him about anything that is on your mind.

....
....
....
....
....
....
....
....
....
....
....
....

Listen for what God is saying to you. Write a letter to yourself from God with what you believe He is saying in response to you.

....
....
....
....
....
....
....
....
....
....
....
....
....
....
....
....
....

5. **Share and Obey** (After devo is completed)—With whom can you share what God spoke to you? If it is direction you received, it is wise to share this with the godly counsel in your life, and if it is revelation or insight, think about who would be encouraged to hear what God has been teaching you and who can hold you accountable to what He spoke.

....
....
....

What steps of obedience or action steps are you going to take?

....
....
....

1. **Time and Place**—When and where did you meet with God?

....

....

....

2. **Be Still and Worship** (5–10 minutes)—Turn on worship music and ask God to help you connect to Him. Start by telling Him how wonderful He is and ask if there is any burden you need to release to Him. After you are finished, write down any impressions, thoughts, or themes you felt during your time of worship.

....

....

....

3. **Read and Pray** (10–15 minutes)—Read the following passage and use the SOAP method and the GOD SPA questions:

> "What, then, shall we say in response to these things? If God is for us, who can be against us? He who did not spare his own Son, but gave him up for us all—how will he not also, along with him, graciously give us all things? Who will bring any charge against those whom God has chosen? It is God who justifies. Who then is the one who condemns? No one. Christ Jesus who died—more than that, who was raised to life—is at the right hand of God and is also interceding for us. Who shall separate us from the love of Christ? Shall trouble or hardship or persecution or famine or nakedness or danger or sword? As it is written: 'For your sake we face death all day long; we are considered as sheep to be slaughtered.' No, in all these things

we are more than conquerors through him who loved us. For I am convinced that neither death nor life, neither angels nor demons, neither the present nor the future, nor any powers, neither height nor depth, nor anything else in all creation, will be able to separate us from the love of God that is in Christ Jesus our Lord." (Romans 8:31–39)

Observation—What stands out to you in this passage?

....

....

....

Application—How can you apply this passage to your life? (You may not have all of these answered for every passage, but it is helpful to ask the following questions.) Is there a/an:

Growth Area?

....

....

....

Obedience Needed?

....

....

....

Direction to Follow?

....

....

....

Sin to Confess?

....

....

....

Promise to Claim?

....

....

....

Accountability?

....

....

....

Prayer—Spend a minute in prayer asking God to help you apply these truths to your life.

4. **Write and Listen** (10–15 minutes)—Write a letter to God. This can be in response to what He was saying to you through Scripture, or you can write Him about anything that is on your mind.

....

....

....

....

....

....

....

....

....

....

....

....

....

....

....

....

....

Listen for what God is saying to you. Write a letter to yourself from God with what you believe He is saying in response to you.

....
....
....
....
....
....
....
....
....
....
....
....
....
....
....
....
....

5. **Share and Obey** (After devo is completed)—With whom can you share what God spoke to you? If it is direction you received, it is wise to share this with the godly counsel in your life, and if it is revelation or insight, think about who would be encouraged to hear what God has been teaching you and who can hold you accountable to what He spoke.

....
....
....

What steps of obedience or action steps are you going to take?

....
....
....

Judges 7:1–8

1. **Time and Place**—When and where did you meet with God?

....

....

....

2. **Be Still and Worship** (5–10 minutes)—Turn on worship music and ask God to help you connect to Him. Start by telling Him how wonderful He is and ask if there is any burden you need to release to Him. After you are finished, write down any impressions, thoughts, or themes you felt during your time of worship.

....

....

....

3. **Read and Pray** (10–15 minutes)—Read the following passage and use the SOAP method and the GOD SPA questions:

> "Early in the morning, Jerub-Baal (that is, Gideon) and all his men camped at the spring of Harod. The camp of Midian was north of them in the valley near the hill of Moreh. The Lord said to Gideon, 'You have too many men. I cannot deliver Midian into their hands, or Israel would boast against me, 'My own strength has saved me.' Now announce to the army, 'Anyone who trembles with fear may turn back and leave Mount Gilead.' So twenty-two thousand men left, while ten thousand remained. But the Lord said to Gideon, 'There are still too many men. Take them down to the water, and I will thin them out for you there. If I say, 'This one shall go with you,' he shall go; but if I say, 'This one shall not go with you,' he shall not go.' So

Gideon took the men down to the water. There the Lord told him, 'Separate those who lap the water with their tongues as a dog laps from those who kneel down to drink.' Three hundred of them drank from cupped hands, lapping like dogs. All the rest got down on their knees to drink. The Lord said to Gideon, 'With the three hundred men that lapped I will save you and give the Midianites into your hands. Let all the others go home.' So Gideon sent the rest of the Israelites home but kept the three hundred, who took over the provisions and trumpets of the others." (Judges 7:1–8)

Observation—What stands out to you in this passage?

....

....

....

Application—How can you apply this passage to your life? (You may not have all of these answered for every passage, but it is helpful to ask the following questions.) Is there a/an:

Growth Area?

....

....

....

Obedience Needed?

....

....

....

Direction to Follow?

....

....

....

Sin to Confess?

....

....

....

Promise to Claim?

....

....

....

Accountability?

....

....

....

Prayer—Spend a minute in prayer asking God to help you apply these truths to your life.

4. **Write and Listen** (10–15 minutes)—Write a letter to God. This can be in response to what He was saying to you through Scripture, or you can write Him about anything that is on your mind.

....

....

....

....

....

....

....

....

....

....

....

....

Listen for what God is saying to you. Write a letter to yourself from God with what you believe He is saying in response to you.

....

....

....

....

....

....

....

....

....

....

....

....

....

....

....

....

....

5. Share and Obey (After devo is completed)—With whom can you share what God spoke to you? If it is direction you received, it is wise to share this with the godly counsel in your life, and if it is revelation or insight, think about who would be encouraged to hear what God has been teaching you and who can hold you accountable to what He spoke.

....

....

....

What steps of obedience or action steps are you going to take?

....

....

....

Acts 9:1–19

1. **Time and Place**—When and where did you meet with God?

....

....

....

2. **Be Still and Worship** (5–10 minutes)—Turn on worship music and ask God to help you connect to Him. Start by telling Him how wonderful He is and ask if there is any burden you need to release to Him. After you are finished, write down any impressions, thoughts, or themes you felt during your time of worship.

....

....

....

3. **Read and Pray** (10–15 minutes)—Read the following passage and use the SOAP method and the GOD SPA questions:

"Meanwhile, Saul was still breathing out murderous threats against the Lord's disciples. He went to the high priest and asked him for letters to the synagogues in Damascus, so that if he found any there who belonged to the Way, whether men or women, he might take them as prisoners to Jerusalem. As he neared Damascus on his journey, suddenly a light from heaven flashed around him. He fell to the ground and heard a voice say to him, 'Saul, Saul, why do you persecute me?' 'Who are you, Lord?' Saul asked. 'I am Jesus, whom you are persecuting,' he replied. 'Now get up and go into the city, and you will be told what you must do.' The men traveling with Saul stood there speechless; they heard the sound but did not see anyone. Saul got up from the ground, but when he opened his eyes he could see nothing. So they led him by the hand into Damascus. For three days he was blind, and did not eat or drink anything. In Damascus there was a disciple named Ananias. The Lord called to him in a vision, 'Ananias!' 'Yes, Lord,' he answered. The Lord told him, 'Go to the house of Judas on Straight Street and ask for a man from Tarsus named Saul, for he is praying. In a vision he has seen a man named Ananias come and place his hands on him to restore his sight.' 'Lord,' Ananias answered, 'I have heard many reports about this man and all the harm he has done to your holy people in Jerusalem. And he has come here with authority from the chief priests to arrest all who call on your name.' But the Lord said to Ananias, 'Go! This man is my chosen instrument to proclaim my name to the Gentiles and their kings and to the people of Israel. I will show him how much he must suffer for my name.' Then Ananias went to the house and entered it. Placing his hands on Saul, he said, 'Brother Saul, the Lord—Jesus, who appeared to you on the road as you were coming here—has sent me so that you may see again and be filled with the Holy Spirit.' Immediately, something like scales fell from Saul's eyes, and he could see again. He got up and was baptized, and after taking some food, he regained his strength." (Acts 9:1–19)

Observation—What stands out to you in this passage?

....
....
....
....
....
....
....

Application—How can you apply this passage to your life? (You may not have all of these answered for every passage, but it is helpful to ask the following questions). Is there a/an:

Growth Area?

....
....
....

Obedience Needed?

....
....
....

Direction to Follow?

....
....
....

Sin to Confess?

....
....
....

Promise to Claim?

....
....
....

Accountability?

....
....
....

Prayer—Spend a minute in prayer asking God to help you apply these truths to your life.

4. **Write and Listen** (10–15 minutes)—Write a letter to God. This can be in response to what He was saying to you through Scripture, or you can write Him about anything that is on your mind.

....
....
....
....
....
....
....
....
....
....
....
....
....
....
....

Listen for what God is saying to you. Write a letter to yourself from God with what you believe He is saying in response to you.

....
....
....
....
....
....
....

....

....

....

....

....

....

....

....

....

5. **Share and Obey** (After devo is completed)—With whom can you share what God spoke to you? If it is direction you received, it is wise to share this with the godly counsel in your life, and if it is revelation or insight, think about who would be encouraged to hear what God has been teaching you and who can hold you accountable to what He spoke.

....

....

....

What steps of obedience or action steps are you going to take?

....

....

....

Ephesians 1:15–23

1. **Time and Place**—When and where did you meet with God?

....

....

....

2. **Be Still and Worship** (5–10 minutes)—Turn on worship music and ask God to help you connect to Him. Start by telling Him how wonderful He is and ask if there is any burden you need to release to Him. After you are finished, write down any impressions, thoughts, or themes you felt during your time of worship.

....

....

....

3. **Read and Pray** (10–15 minutes)—Read the following passage and use the SOAP method and the GOD SPA questions:

> "For this reason, ever since I heard about your faith in the Lord Jesus and your love for all God's people, I have not stopped giving thanks for you, remembering you in my prayers. I keep asking that the God of our Lord Jesus Christ, the glorious Father, may give you the Spirit of wisdom and revelation, so that you may know him better. I pray that the eyes of your heart may be enlightened in order that you may know the hope to which He has called you, the riches of his glorious inheritance in His holy people, and His incomparably great power for us who believe. That power is the same as the mighty strength He exerted when He raised Christ from the dead and seated Him at his right hand in the heavenly realms, far above all rule

and authority, power and dominion, and every name that is invoked, not only in the present age but also in the one to come. And God placed all things under His feet and appointed him to be head over everything for the church, which is His body, the fullness of Him who fills everything in every way." (Ephesians 1:15–23)

Observation—What stands out to you in this passage?

....

....

....

Application—How can you apply this passage to your life? (You may not have all of these answered for every passage, but it is helpful to ask the following questions). Is there a/an:

Growth Area?

....

....

....

Obedience Needed?

....

....

....

Direction to Follow?

....

....

....

Sin to Confess?

....

....

....

Promise to Claim?

....

....

....

Accountability?

....

....

....

Prayer—Spend a minute in prayer asking God to help you apply these truths to your life.

4. **Write and Listen** (10–15 minutes)—Write a letter to God. This can be in response to what He was saying to you through Scripture, or you can write Him about anything that is on your mind.

....

....

....

....

....

....

....

....

....

....

....

....

....

....

....

Listen for what God is saying to you. Write a letter to yourself from God with what you believe He is saying in response to you.

....

....

....

....

....

....

....

....

....

....

....

....

....

....

5. **Share and Obey** (After devo is completed)—With whom can you share what God spoke to you? If it is direction you received, it is wise to share this with the godly counsel in your life, and if it is revelation or insight, think about who would be encouraged to hear what God has been teaching you and who can hold you accountable to what He spoke.

....

....

....

What steps of obedience or action steps are you going to take?

....

....

....

Deuteronomy 8:1-11

1. **Time and Place**—When and where did you meet with God?

....

....

....

2. **Be Still and Worship** (5–10 minutes)—Turn on worship music and ask God to help you connect to Him. Start by telling Him how wonderful He is and ask if there is any burden you need to release to Him. After you are finished, write down any impressions, thoughts, or themes you felt during your time of worship.

....

....

....

3. **Read and Pray** (10–15 minutes)—Read the following passage and use the SOAP method and the GOD SPA questions:

> "Be careful to follow every command I am giving you today, so that you may live and increase and may enter and possess the land the Lord promised on oath to your ancestors. Remember how the Lord your God led you all the way in the wilderness these forty years, to humble and test you in order to know what was in your heart, whether or not you would keep his commands. He humbled you, causing you to hunger and then feeding you with manna, which neither you nor your ancestors had known, to teach you that man does not live on bread alone but on every word that comes from the mouth of the Lord. Your clothes did not wear out and your feet did not swell during these forty years. Know then in your heart that as a man

disciplines his son, so the Lord your God disciplines you. Observe the commands of the Lord your God, walking in obedience to him and revering him. For the Lord your God is bringing you into a good land—a land with brooks, streams, and deep springs gushing out into the valleys and hills; a land with wheat and barley, vines and fig trees, pomegranates, olive oil and honey; a land where bread will not be scarce and you will lack nothing; a land where the rocks are iron and you can dig copper out of the hills. When you have eaten and are satisfied, praise the Lord your God for the good land He has given you. Be careful that you do not forget the Lord your God, failing to observe his commands, His laws and His decrees that I am giving you this day." (Deuteronomy 8:1–11)

Observation—What stands out to you in this passage?

....

....

....

....

....

Application—How can you apply this passage to your life? (You may not have all of these answered for every passage, but it is helpful to ask the following questions). Is there a/an:

Growth Area?

....

....

....

Obedience Needed?

....

....

....

Direction to Follow?

....
....
....

Sin to Confess?

....
....
....

Promise to Claim?

....
....
....

Accountability?

....
....
....

Prayer—Spend a minute in prayer asking God to help you apply these truths to your life.

4. **Write and Listen** (10–15 minutes)—Write a letter to God. This can be in response to what He was saying to you through Scripture, or you can write Him about anything that is on your mind.

....
....
....
....
....
....
....

....
....
....
....
....
....
....
....

Listen for what God is saying to you. Write a letter to yourself from God with what you believe He is saying in response to you.

....
....
....
....
....
....
....
....
....
....
....
....
....
....
....
....

5. **Share and Obey** (After devo is completed)—With whom can you share what God spoke to you? If it is direction you received, it is wise to share this with the godly counsel in your life, and if it is revelation or in-

sight, think about who would be encouraged to hear what God has been teaching you and who can hold you accountable to what He spoke.

....

....

....

What steps of obedience or action steps are you going to take?

....

....

....

Proverbs 3:1–6

1. **Time and Place**—When and where did you meet with God?

....

....

....

2. **Be Still and Worship** (5–10 minutes)—Turn on worship music and ask God to help you connect to Him. Start by telling Him how wonderful He is and ask if there is any burden you need to release to Him. After you are finished, write down any impressions, thoughts, or themes you felt during your time of worship.

....

....

....

3. **Read and Pray** (10–15 minutes)—Read the following passage and use the SOAP method and the GOD SPA questions:

> "My son, do not forget my teaching, but keep my commands in your heart, for they will prolong your life many years and bring you peace and prosperity. Let love and faithfulness never leave you; bind them around your neck, write them on the tablet of your heart. Then you will win favor and a good name in the sight of God and man. Trust in the Lord with all your heart and lean not on your own understanding; in all your ways submit to him, and he will make your paths straight." (Proverbs 3:1–6)

Observation—What stands out to you in this passage?

....
....
....
....

Application—How can you apply this passage to your life? (You may not have all of these answered for every passage, but it is helpful to ask the following questions.) Is there a/an:

Growth Area?

....
....
....

Obedience Needed?

....
....
....

Direction to Follow?

....
....
....

Sin to Confess?

....
....
....

Promise to Claim?

....
....
....

Accountability?

....

....

....

Prayer—Spend a minute in prayer asking God to help you apply these truths to your life.

4. **Write and Listen** (10–15 minutes)—Write a letter to God. This can be in response to what He was saying to you through Scripture, or you can write Him about anything that is on your mind.

....
....
....
....
....
....
....
....
....
....
....
....
....
....
....
....
....
....
....
....
....
....
....

Listen for what God is saying to you. Write a letter to yourself from God with what you believe He is saying in response to you.

....

....

....

....

....

....

....

....

....

....

....

....

....

....

....

....

5. **Share and Obey** (After devo is completed)—With whom can you share what God spoke to you? If it is direction you received, it is wise to share this with the godly counsel in your life, and if it is revelation or insight, think about who would be encouraged to hear what God has been teaching you and who can hold you accountable to what He spoke.

....

....

....

What steps of obedience or action steps are you going to take?

....

....

....

John 15:9–17

1. **Time and Place**—When and where did you meet with God?

....

....

....

2. **Be Still and Worship** (5–10 minutes)—Turn on worship music and ask God to help you connect to Him. Start by telling Him how wonderful He is and ask if there is any burden you need to release to Him. After you are finished, write down any impressions, thoughts, or themes you felt during your time of worship.

....

....

....

3. **Read and Pray** (10–15 minutes)—Read the following passage and use the SOAP method and the GOD SPA questions:

> "As the Father has loved me, so have I loved you. Now remain in my love. If you keep my commands, you will remain in my love, just as I have kept my Father's commands and remain in his love. I have told you this so that my joy may be in you and that your joy may be complete. My command is this: Love each other as I have loved you. Greater love has no one than this: to lay down one's life for one's friends. You are my friends if you do what I command. I no longer call you servants, because a servant does not know his master's business. Instead, I have called you friends, for everything that I learned from my Father I have made known to you. You did not choose me, but I chose you and appointed you so that you might go and bear

fruit—fruit that will last—and so that whatever you ask in my name the Father will give you. This is my command: Love each other." (John 15:9–17)

Observation—What stands out to you in this passage?

....
....
....
....
....

Application—How can you apply this passage to your life? (You may not have all of these answered for every passage, but it is helpful to ask the following questions.) Is there a/an:

Growth Area?

....
....
....

Obedience Needed?

....
....
....

Direction to Follow?

....
....
....

Sin to Confess?

....
....
....

Promise to Claim?

....
....
....

Accountability?

....
....
....

Prayer—Spend a minute in prayer asking God to help you apply these truths to your life.

4. **Write and Listen** (10–15 minutes)—Write a letter to God. This can be in response to what He was saying to you through Scripture, or you can write Him about anything that is on your mind.

....
....
....
....
....
....
....
....
....
....
....
....
....
....

Listen for what God is saying to you. Write a letter to yourself from God with what you believe He is saying in response to you.

....
....
....
....
....
....
....
....
....
....
....
....
....
....
....
....
....

5. **Share and Obey** (After devo is completed)—With whom can you share what God spoke to you? If it is direction you received, it is wise to share this with the godly counsel in your life, and if it is revelation or insight, think about who would be encouraged to hear what God has been teaching you and who can hold you accountable to what He spoke.

....
....
....

What steps of obedience or action steps are you going to take?

....
....
....

1 Samuel 3:1–11

1. **Time and Place**—When and where did you meet with God?

....

....

....

2. **Be Still and Worship** (5–10 minutes)—Turn on worship music and ask God to help you connect to Him. Start by telling Him how wonderful He is and ask if there is any burden you need to release to Him. After you are finished, write down any impressions, thoughts, or themes you felt during your time of worship.

....

....

....

3. **Read and Pray** (10–15 minutes)—Read the following passage and use the SOAP method and the GOD SPA questions:

"The boy Samuel ministered before the Lord under Eli. In those days the word of the Lord was rare; there were not many visions. One night Eli, whose eyes were becoming so weak that he could barely see, was lying down in his usual place. The lamp of God had not yet gone out, and Samuel was lying down in the house of the Lord, where the ark of God was. Then the Lord called Samuel. Samuel answered, 'Here I am.' And he ran to Eli and said, 'Here I am; you called me.' But Eli said, 'I did not call; go back and lie down.' So he went and lay down. Again the Lord called, 'Samuel!' And Samuel got up and went to Eli and said, 'Here I am; you called me.' 'My son,' Eli said, 'I did not call; go back and lie down.' Now Samuel did not yet know the Lord: The word of the Lord had not yet been revealed to him. A third time the Lord called, 'Samuel!' And Samuel got up and went to Eli and said, 'Here I am; you called me.' Then Eli realized that the Lord was calling the boy. So Eli told Samuel, 'Go and lie down, and if he calls you, say, 'Speak, Lord, for your servant is listening.'" So Samuel went and lay down in his place. The Lord came and stood there, calling as at the other times, 'Samuel! Samuel!' Then Samuel said, 'Speak, for your servant is listening.' And the Lord said to Samuel: 'See, I am about to do something in Israel that will make the ears of everyone who hears about it tingle.'" (1 Samuel 3:1–11)

Observation—What stands out to you in this passage?

....

....

....

Application—How can you apply this passage to your life? (You may not have all of these answered for every passage, but it is helpful to ask the following questions.) Is there a/an:

Growth Area?

....

....

Obedience Needed?

....

....

....

Direction to Follow?

....

....

Sin to Confess?

....

....

....

Promise to Claim?

....

....

....

Accountability?

....

....

....

Prayer—Spend a minute in prayer asking God to help you apply these truths to your life.

4. **Write and Listen** (10–15 minutes)—Write a letter to God. This can be in response to what He was saying to you through Scripture or you can write Him about anything that is on your mind.

....

....

....

....

....

....

....

....

....

....

....

....

....
....
....
....
....
....
....
....
....
....

Listen for what God is saying to you. Write a letter to yourself from God with what you believe He is saying in response to you.

....
....
....
....
....
....
....
....
....
....
....
....
....
....
....
....
....

5. **Share and Obey** (After devo is completed)—With whom can you share what God spoke to you? If it is direction you received, it is wise to share this with the godly counsel in your life, and if it is revelation or in-

sight, think about who would be encouraged to hear what God has been teaching you and who can hold you accountable to what He spoke.

....

....

....

What steps of obedience or action steps are you going to take?

....

....

....

1. **Time and Place**—When and where did you meet with God?

....

....

....

2. **Be Still and Worship** (5–10 minutes)—Turn on worship music and ask God to help you connect to Him. Start by telling Him how wonderful He is and ask if there is any burden you need to release to Him. After you are finished, write down any impressions, thoughts, or themes you felt during your time of worship.

....

....

....

3. **Read and Pray** (10–15 minutes)—Read the following passage and use the SOAP method and the GOD SPA questions:

> "As Jesus and his disciples were on their way, he came to a village where a woman named Martha opened her home to him. She had a sister called Mary, who sat at the Lord's feet listening to what he said. But Martha was distracted by all the preparations that had to be made. She came to him and asked, 'Lord, don't you care that my sister has left me to do the work by myself? Tell her to help me!' 'Martha, Martha,' the Lord answered, 'you are worried and upset about many things, but few things are needed—or indeed only one. Mary has chosen what is better, and it will not be taken away from her.'" (Luke 10:38–42)

Observation—What stands out to you in this passage?

....
....
....
....

Application—How can you apply this passage to your life? (You may not have all of these answered for every passage, but it is helpful to ask the following questions.) Is there a/an:

Growth Area?

....
....
....

Obedience Needed?

....
....
....

Direction to Follow?

....
....
....

Sin to Confess?

....
....
....

Promise to Claim?

....
....
....

Accountability?

....
....
....

Prayer—Spend a minute in prayer asking God to help you apply these truths to your life.

4. **Write and Listen** (10–15 minutes)—Write a letter to God. This can be in response to what He was saying to you through Scripture, or you can write Him about anything that is on your mind.

....
....
....
....
....
....
....
....
....
....
....
....
....
....
....
....
....
....
....
....

Listen for what God is saying to you. Write a letter to yourself from God with what you believe He is saying in response to you.

....

....

....

....

....

....

....

....

....

....

....

....

....

....

....

5. **Share and Obey** (After devo is completed)—With whom can you share what God spoke to you? If it is direction you received, it is wise to share this with the godly counsel in your life, and if it is revelation or insight, think about who would be encouraged to hear what God has been teaching you and who can hold you accountable to what He spoke.

....

....

....

What steps of obedience or action steps are you going to take?

....

....

....

1. **Time and Place**—When and where did you meet with God?

....

....

....

2. **Be Still and Worship** (5–10 minutes)—Turn on worship music and ask God to help you connect to Him. Start by telling Him how wonderful He is and ask if there is any burden you need to release to Him. After you are finished, write down any impressions, thoughts, or themes you felt during your time of worship.

....

....

....

....

3. **Read and Pray** (10–15 minutes)—Read the following passage and use the SOAP method and the GOD SPA questions:

> "Blessed is the one who does not walk in step with the wicked or stand in the way that sinners take or sit in the company of mockers, but whose delight is in the law of the Lord, and who meditates on his law day and night. That person is like a tree planted by streams of water, which yields its fruit in season and whose leaf does not wither—whatever they do prospers. Not so the wicked! They are like chaff that the wind blows away. Therefore the wicked will not stand in the judgment, nor sinners in the assembly of the righteous. For the Lord watches over the way of the righteous, but the way of the wicked leads to destruction." (Psalm 1:1–6)

Observation—What stands out to you in this passage?

....

....

....

....

Application—How can you apply this passage to your life? (You may not have all of these answered for every passage, but it is helpful to ask the following questions.) Is there a/an:

Growth Area?

....

....

....

Obedience Needed?

....

....

....

Direction to Follow?

....

....

....

Sin to Confess?

....

....

....

Promise to Claim?

....

....

....

Accountability?

....

....

....

Prayer—Spend a minute in prayer asking God to help you apply these truths to your life.

4. **Write and Listen** (10–15 minutes)—Write a letter to God. This can be in response to what He was saying to you through Scripture, or you can write Him about anything that is on your mind.

....

....

....

....

....

....

....

....

....

....

....

....

....

....

....

....

....

....

....

....

....

Listen for what God is saying to you. Write a letter to yourself from God with what you believe He is saying in response to you.

....
....
....
....
....
....
....
....
....
....
....
....
....
....
....
....

5. **Share and Obey** (After devo is completed)—With whom can you share what God spoke to you? If it is direction you received, it is wise to share this with the godly counsel in your life, and if it is revelation or insight, think about who would be encouraged to hear what God has been teaching you and who can hold you accountable to what He spoke.

....
....
....

What steps of obedience or action steps are you going to take?

....
....
....

Matthew 6:25–33

1. **Time and Place**—When and where did you meet with God?

....

....

....

2. **Be Still and Worship** (5–10 minutes)—Turn on worship music and
ask God to help you connect to Him. Start by telling Him how wonderful
He is and ask if there is any burden you need to release to Him. After you
are finished, write down any impressions, thoughts, or themes you felt
during your time of worship.

....

....

....

3. **Read and Pray** (10–15 minutes)—Read the following passage and use
the SOAP method and the GOD SPA questions:

> "Therefore I tell you, do not worry about your life, what you
> will eat or drink; or about your body, what you will wear. Is not
> life more than food, and the body more than clothes? Look at
> the birds of the air; they do not sow or reap or store away in
> barns, and yet your heavenly Father feeds them. Are you not
> much more valuable than they? Can any one of you by wor-
> rying add a single hour to your life? And why do you worry
> about clothes? See how the flowers of the field grow. They do
> not labor or spin. Yet I tell you that not even Solomon in all
> his splendor was dressed like one of these. If that is how God
> clothes the grass of the field, which is here today and tomorrow
> is thrown into the fire, will he not much more clothe you—you

of little faith? So do not worry, saying, 'What shall we eat?' or 'What shall we drink?' or 'What shall we wear?' For the pagans run after all these things, and your heavenly Father knows that you need them. But seek first his kingdom and his righteousness, and all these things will be given to you as well." (Matthew 6:25–33)

Observation—What stands out to you in this passage?

....
....
....

Application—How can you apply this passage to your life? (You may not have all of these answered for every passage, but it is helpful to ask the following questions.) Is there a/an:

Growth Area?

....
....
....

Obedience Needed?

....
....
....

Direction to Follow?

....
....
....

Sin to Confess?

....
....
....

Promise to Claim?

....

....

....

Accountability?

....

....

....

Prayer—Spend a minute in prayer asking God to help you apply these truths to your life.

4. **Write and Listen** (10–15 minutes)—Write a letter to God. This can be in response to what He was saying to you through Scripture, or you can write Him about anything that is on your mind.

....

....

....

....

....

....

....

....

....

....

....

....

....

....

....

....

....

....

Listen for what God is saying to you. Write a letter to yourself from God with what you believe He is saying in response to you.

....
....
....
....
....
....
....
....
....
....
....
....
....
....
....
....

5. **Share and Obey** (After devo is completed)—With whom can you share what God spoke to you? If it is direction you received, it is wise to share this with the godly counsel in your life, and if it is revelation or insight, think about who would be encouraged to hear what God has been teaching you and who can hold you accountable to what He spoke.

....
....
....

What steps of obedience or action steps are you going to take?

....
....
....

1. **Time and Place**—When and where did you meet with God?

....

....

....

2. **Be Still and Worship** (5–10 minutes)—Turn on worship music and ask God to help you connect to Him. Start by telling Him how wonderful He is and ask if there is any burden you need to release to Him. After you are finished, write down any impressions, thoughts, or themes you felt during your time of worship.

....

....

....

3. **Read and Pray** (10–15 minutes)—Read the following passage and use the SOAP method and the GOD SPA questions:

"When Esther's words were reported to Mordecai, he sent back this answer: 'Do not think that because you are in the king's house you alone of all the Jews will escape. For if you remain silent at this time, relief and deliverance for the Jews will arise from another place, but you and your father's family will perish. And who knows but that you have come to your royal position for such a time as this?' Then Esther sent this reply to Mordecai: 'Go, gather together all the Jews who are in Susa, and fast for me. Do not eat or drink for three days, night or day. I and my attendants will fast as you do. When this is done, I will go to the king, even though it is against the law. And if I perish, I perish.'" (Esther 4:12–16)

Observation—What stands out to you in this passage?

....
....
....
....

Application—How can you apply this passage to your life? (You may not have all of these answered for every passage, but it is helpful to ask the following questions.) Is there a/an:

Growth Area?

....
....
....

Obedience Needed?

....
....
....

Direction to Follow?

....
....
....

Sin to Confess?

....
....
....

Promise to Claim?

....
....
....

Accountability?

....

....

....

Prayer—Spend a minute in prayer asking God to help you apply these truths to your life.

4. **Write and Listen** (10–15 minutes)—Write a letter to God. This can be in response to what He was saying to you through Scripture, or you can write Him about anything that is on your mind.

....

....

....

....

....

....

....

....

....

....

....

....

....

....

....

....

....

....

....

....

....

....

Listen for what God is saying to you. Write a letter to yourself from God with what you believe He is saying in response to you.

....

....

....

....

....

....

....

....

....

....

....

....

....

....

....

....

5. **Share and Obey** (After devo is completed)—With whom can you share what God spoke to you? If it is direction you received, it is wise to share this with the godly counsel in your life, and if it is revelation or insight, think about who would be encouraged to hear what God has been teaching you and who can hold you accountable to what He spoke.

....

....

....

What steps of obedience or action steps are you going to take?

....

....

....

Nehemiah 2:17–20

1. **Time and Place**—When and where did you meet with God?

....

....

....

2. **Be Still and Worship** (5–10 minutes)—Turn on worship music and ask God to help you connect to Him. Start by telling Him how wonderful He is and ask if there is any burden you need to release to Him. After you are finished, write down any impressions, thoughts, or themes you felt during your time of worship.

....

....

....

....

3. **Read and Pray** (10–15 minutes)—Read the following passage and use the SOAP method and the GOD SPA questions:

> "Then Nehemiah said to them, 'You see the trouble we are in: Jerusalem lies in ruins, and its gates have been burned with fire. Come, let us rebuild the wall of Jerusalem, and we will no longer be in disgrace.' I also told them about the gracious hand of my God on me and what the king had said to me. They replied, 'Let us start rebuilding.' So they began this good work. But when Sanballat the Horonite, Tobiah the Ammonite official and Geshem the Arab heard about it, they mocked and ridiculed us. 'What is this you are doing?' they asked. 'Are you rebelling against the king?' I answered them by saying, 'The God of heaven will give us success. We his servants will start

rebuilding, but as for you, you have no share in Jerusalem or any claim or historic right to it.' " (Nehemiah 2:17–20)

Observation—What stands out to you in this passage?

....
....
....
....
....
....

Application—How can you apply this passage to your life? (You may not have all of these answered for every passage, but it is helpful to ask the following questions.) Is there a/an:

Growth Area?

....
....
....

Obedience Needed?

....
....
....

Direction to Follow?

....
....
....

Sin to Confess?

....
....
....

Promise to Claim?

....

....

....

Accountability?

....

....

....

Prayer—Spend a minute in prayer asking God to help you apply these truths to your life.

4. **Write and Listen** (10–15 minutes)—Write a letter to God. This can be in response to what He was saying to you through Scripture, or you can write Him about anything that is on your mind.

....

....

....

....

....

....

....

....

....

....

....

....

....

....

....

....

....

Listen for what God is saying to you. Write a letter to yourself from God with what you believe He is saying in response to you.

....

....

....

....

....

....

....

....

....

....

....

....

....

....

....

5. **Share and Obey** (After devo is completed)—With whom can you share what God spoke to you? If it is direction you received, it is wise to share this with the godly counsel in your life, and if it is revelation or insight, think about who would be encouraged to hear what God has been teaching you and who can hold you accountable to what He spoke.

....

....

....

What steps of obedience or action steps are you going to take?

....

....

....

Mark 4:35–41

1. **Time and Place**—When and where did you meet with God?

....

....

....

2. **Be Still and Worship** (5–10 minutes)—Turn on worship music and ask God to help you connect to Him. Start by telling Him how wonderful He is and ask if there is any burden you need to release to Him. After you are finished, write down any impressions, thoughts, or themes you felt during your time of worship.

....

....

....

3. **Read and Pray** (10–15 minutes)—Read the following passage and use the SOAP method and the GOD SPA questions:

"That day when evening came, He said to His disciples, 'Let us go over to the other side.' Leaving the crowd behind, they took him along, just as he was, in the boat. There were also other boats with him. A furious squall came up, and the waves broke over the boat, so that it was nearly swamped. Jesus was in the stern, sleeping on a cushion. The disciples woke him and said to him, 'Teacher, don't you care if we drown?' He got up, rebuked the wind and said to the waves, 'Quiet! Be still!' Then the wind died down and it was completely calm. He said to his disciples, 'Why are you so afraid? Do you still have no faith?' They were terrified and asked each other, 'Who is this? Even the wind and the waves obey him!'" (Mark 4:35–41)

Observation—What stands out to you in this passage?

....
....
....
....

Application—How can you apply this passage to your life? (You may not have all of these answered for every passage, but it is helpful to ask the following questions). Is there a/an:

Growth Area?

....
....
....

Obedience Needed?

....
....
....

Direction to Follow?

....
....
....

Sin to Confess?

....
....
....

Promise to Claim?

....
....
....

Accountability?

....

....

....

Prayer—Spend a minute in prayer asking God to help you apply these truths to your life.

4. **Write and Listen** (10–15 minutes)—Write a letter to God. This can be in response to what He was saying to you through Scripture, or you can write Him about anything that is on your mind.

....

....

....

....

....

....

....

....

....

....

....

....

....

....

....

....

....

....

....

....

....

Listen for what God is saying to you. Write a letter to yourself from God with what you believe He is saying in response to you.

....
....
....
....
....
....
....
....
....
....
....
....
....
....
....
....
....

5. **Share and Obey** (After devo is completed)—With whom can you share what God spoke to you? If it is direction you received, it is wise to share this with the godly counsel in your life, and if it is revelation or insight, think about who would be encouraged to hear what God has been teaching you and who can hold you accountable to what He spoke.

....
....
....

What steps of obedience or action steps are you going to take?

....
....
....

1. **Time and Place**—When and where did you meet with God?

....

....

....

2. **Be Still and Worship** (5–10 minutes)—Turn on worship music and ask God to help you connect to Him. Start by telling Him how wonderful He is and ask if there is any burden you need to release to Him. After you are finished, write down any impressions, thoughts, or themes you felt during your time of worship.

....

....

....

3. **Read and Pray** (10–15 minutes)—Read the following passage and use the SOAP method and the GOD SPA questions:

> "Now faith is confidence in what we hope for and assurance about what we do not see. This is what the ancients were commended for. By faith we understand that the universe was formed at God's command, so that what is seen was not made out of what was visible. By faith Abel brought God a better offering than Cain did. By faith he was commended as righteous, when God spoke well of his offerings. And by faith Abel still speaks, even though he is dead. By faith Enoch was taken from this life, so that he did not experience death: 'He could not be found, because God had taken him away.' For before he was taken, he was commended as one who pleased God. And without faith it is impossible to please God, because anyone who

comes to him must believe that he exists and that he rewards those who earnestly seek him." (Hebrews 11:1–6)

Observation—What stands out to you in this passage?

....

....

....

Application—How can you apply this passage to your life? (You may not have all of these answered for every passage, but it is helpful to ask the following questions.) Is there a/an:

Growth Area?

....

....

....

Obedience Needed?

....

....

....

Direction to Follow?

....

....

....

Sin to Confess?

....

....

....

Promise to Claim?

....

....

Accountability?

....
....
....

Prayer—Spend a minute in prayer asking God to help you apply these truths to your life.

4. **Write and Listen** (10–15 minutes)—Write a letter to God. This can be in response to what He was saying to you through Scripture, or you can write Him about anything that is on your mind.

....
....
....
....
....
....
....
....
....
....
....
....
....
....
....
....
....
....
....
....
....
....

Listen for what God is saying to you. Write a letter to yourself from God with what you believe He is saying in response to you.

....
....
....
....
....
....
....
....
....
....
....
....
....
....
....

5. **Share and Obey** (After devo is completed)—With whom can you share what God spoke to you? If it is direction you received, it is wise to share this with the godly counsel in your life, and if it is revelation or insight, think about who would be encouraged to hear what God has been teaching you and who can hold you accountable to what He spoke.

....
....
....

What steps of obedience or action steps are you going to take?

....
....
....

1. **Time and Place**—When and where did you meet with God?

....

....

....

2. **Be Still and Worship** (5–10 minutes)—Turn on worship music and ask God to help you connect to Him. Start by telling Him how wonderful He is and ask if there is any burden you need to release to Him. After you are finished, write down any impressions, thoughts, or themes you felt during your time of worship.

....

....

....

....

3. **Read and Pray** (10–15 minutes)—Read the following passage and use the SOAP method and the GOD SPA questions:

> "The Lord is my shepherd; I lack nothing. He makes me lie down in green pastures, He leads me beside quiet waters, He refreshes my soul. He guides me along the right paths for His name's sake. Even though I walk through the darkest valley, I will fear no evil, for you are with me; your rod and your staff, they comfort me. You prepare a table before me in the presence of my enemies. You anoint my head with oil; my cup overflows. Surely your goodness and love will follow me all the days of my life, and I will dwell in the house of the Lord forever." (Psalm 23:1–6)

Observation—What stands out to you in this passage?

....
....
....
....

Application—How can you apply this passage to your life? (You may not have all of these answered for every passage, but it is helpful to ask the following questions.) Is there a/an:

Growth Area?

....
....
....

Obedience Needed?

....
....
....

Direction to Follow?

....
....
....

Sin to Confess?

....
....
....

Promise to Claim?

....
....
....

Accountability?

....

....

....

Prayer—Spend a minute in prayer asking God to help you apply these truths to your life.

4. **Write and Listen** (10–15 minutes)—Write a letter to God. This can be in response to what He was saying to you through Scripture, or you can write Him about anything that is on your mind.

....

....

....

....

....

....

....

....

....

....

....

....

....

....

....

....

....

....

....

....

Listen for what God is saying to you. Write a letter to yourself from God with what you believe He is saying in response to you.

....
....
....
....
....
....
....
....
....
....
....
....
....
....
....
....
....
....

5. **Share and Obey** (After devo is completed)—With whom can you share what God spoke to you? If it is direction you received, it is wise to share this with the godly counsel in your life, and if it is revelation or insight, think about who would be encouraged to hear what God has been teaching you and who can hold you accountable to what He spoke.

....
....
....

What steps of obedience or action steps are you going to take?

....
....
....

Philippians 4:4–9

1. **Time and Place**—When and where did you meet with God?

....

....

....

2. **Be Still and Worship** (5–10 minutes)—Turn on worship music and ask God to help you connect to Him. Start by telling Him how wonderful He is and ask if there is any burden you need to release to Him. After you are finished, write down any impressions, thoughts, or themes you felt during your time of worship.

....

....

....

3. **Read and Pray** (10–15 minutes)—Read the following passage and use the SOAP method and the GOD SPA questions:

> "Rejoice in the Lord always. I will say it again: Rejoice! Let your gentleness be evident to all. The Lord is near. Do not be anxious about anything, but in every situation, by prayer and petition, with thanksgiving, present your requests to God. And the peace of God, which transcends all understanding, will guard your hearts and your minds in Christ Jesus. Finally, brothers and sisters, whatever is true, whatever is noble, whatever is right, whatever is pure, whatever is lovely, whatever is admirable—if anything is excellent or praiseworthy—think about such things. Whatever you have learned or received or heard from me, or seen in me—put it into practice. And the God of peace will be with you." (Philippians 4:4–9)

Observation—What stands out to you in this passage?

....

....

....

....

Application—How can you apply this passage to your life? (You may not have all of these answered for every passage, but it is helpful to ask the following questions.) Is there a/an:

Growth Area?

....

....

....

Obedience Needed?

....

....

....

Direction to Follow?

....

....

....

Sin to Confess?

....

....

....

Promise to Claim?

....

....

....

Accountability?

....
....
....

Prayer—Spend a minute in prayer asking God to help you apply these truths to your life.

4. **Write and Listen** (10–15 minutes)—Write a letter to God. This can be in response to what He was saying to you through Scripture, or you can write Him about anything that is on your mind.

....
....
....
....
....
....
....
....
....
....
....
....
....
....
....
....
....
....
....
....

Listen for what God is saying to you. Write a letter to yourself from God with what you believe He is saying in response to you.

....
....
....
....
....
....
....
....
....
....
....
....
....
....
....

5. **Share and Obey** (After devo is completed)—With whom can you share what God spoke to you? If it is direction you received, it is wise to share this with the godly counsel in your life, and if it is revelation or insight, think about who would be encouraged to hear what God has been teaching you and who can hold you accountable to what He spoke.

....
....
....

What steps of obedience or action steps are you going to take?

....
....
....

1. **Time and Place**—When and where did you meet with God?

....

....

....

2. **Be Still and Worship** (5–10 minutes)—Turn on worship music and ask God to help you connect to Him. Start by telling Him how wonderful He is and ask if there is any burden you need to release to Him. After you are finished, write down any impressions, thoughts, or themes you felt during your time of worship.

....

....

....

3. **Read and Pray** (10–15 minutes)—Read the following passage and use the SOAP method and the GOD SPA questions:

"In the year that King Uzziah died, I saw the Lord, high and exalted, seated on a throne; and the train of his robe filled the temple. Above him were seraphim, each with six wings: With two wings they covered their faces, with two they covered their feet, and with two they were flying. And they were calling to one another: 'Holy, holy, holy is the Lord Almighty; the whole earth is full of His glory.' At the sound of their voices the doorposts and thresholds shook and the temple was filled with smoke. 'Woe to me!' I cried. 'I am ruined! For I am a man of unclean lips, and I live among a people of unclean lips, and my eyes have seen the King, the Lord Almighty.' Then one of the seraphim flew to me with a live coal in his hand, which he had taken with tongs from the altar. With it he touched my mouth and said, 'See, this has touched your lips; your guilt is taken away and your sin atoned for.' Then I heard the voice of the Lord saying, 'Whom shall I send? And who will go for us?' And I said, 'Here am I. Send me!'" (Isaiah 6:1–8)

Observation—What stands out to you in this passage?

....

....

....

....

Application—How can you apply this passage to your life? (You may not have all of these answered for every passage, but it is helpful to ask the following questions.) Is there a/an:

Growth Area?

....

....

....

Obedience Needed?

....

....

....

Direction to Follow?

....

....

....

Sin to Confess?

....

....

....

Promise to Claim?

....

....

....

Accountability?

....

....

....

Prayer—Spend a minute in prayer asking God to help you apply these truths to your life.

4. **Write and Listen** (10–15 minutes)—Write a letter to God. This can be in response to what He was saying to you through Scripture, or you can write Him about anything that is on your mind.

....

....

....

....

....

....

....

....

....

....

....

....

....

....

....

....

....

....

....

Listen for what God is saying to you. Write a letter to yourself from God with what you believe He is saying in response to you.

....

....

....

....

....

....

....

....

....

....

....

....

....

....

....

....

....

5. **Share and Obey** (After devo is completed)—With whom can you share what God spoke to you? If it is direction you received, it is wise to share this with the godly counsel in your life, and if it is revelation or insight, think about who would be encouraged to hear what God has been teaching you and who can hold you accountable to what He spoke.

....

....

....

What steps of obedience or action steps are you going to take?

....

....

....

John 21:4–14

1. **Time and Place**—When and where did you meet with God?

....

....

....

2. **Be Still and Worship** (5–10 minutes)—Turn on worship music and ask God to help you connect to Him. Start by telling Him how wonderful He is and ask if there is any burden you need to release to Him. After you are finished, write down any impressions, thoughts, or themes you felt during your time of worship.

....

....

....

3. **Read and Pray** (10–15 minutes)—Read the following passage and use the SOAP method and the GOD SPA questions:

"Early in the morning, Jesus stood on the shore, but the disciples did not realize that it was Jesus. He called out to them, 'Friends, haven't you any fish?' 'No,' they answered. He said, 'Throw your net on the right side of the boat and you will find some.' When they did, they were unable to haul the net in because of the large number of fish. Then the disciple whom Jesus loved said to Peter, 'It is the Lord!' As soon as Simon Peter heard him say, 'It is the Lord,' he wrapped his outer garment around him (for he had taken it off) and jumped into the water. The other disciples followed in the boat, towing the net full of fish, for they were not far from shore, about a hundred yards. When they landed, they saw a fire of burning coals there with fish on it, and some bread. Jesus said to them, 'Bring some of the fish you have just caught.' So Simon Peter climbed back into the boat and dragged the net ashore. It was full of large fish, but even with so many the net was not torn. Jesus said to them, 'Come and have breakfast.' None of the disciples dared ask him, 'Who are you?' They knew it was the Lord. Jesus came, took the bread and gave it to them, and did the same with the fish. This was now the third time Jesus appeared to his disciples after he was raised from the dead." (John 21:4–14)

Observation—What stands out to you in this passage?

....

....

....

....

Application—How can you apply this passage to your life? (You may not have all of these answered for every passage, but it is helpful to ask the following questions.) Is there a/an:

Growth Area?

....

....

....

Obedience Needed?

....

....

....

Direction to Follow?

....

....

....

Sin to Confess?

....

....

....

Promise to Claim?

....

....

....

Accountability?

....

....

....

Prayer—Spend a minute in prayer asking God to help you apply these truths to your life.

4. **Write and Listen** (10–15 minutes)—Write a letter to God. This can be in response to what He was saying to you through Scripture, or you can write Him about anything that is on your mind.

....

....

....

....

....

....

....

....

....

....

....

....

Listen for what God is saying to you. Write a letter to yourself from God with what you believe He is saying in response to you.

....
....
....
....
....
....
....
....
....
....
....
....
....
....
....

5. **Share and Obey** (After devo is completed)—With whom can you share what God spoke to you? If it is direction you received, it is wise to share this with the godly counsel in your life, and if it is revelation or insight, think about who would be encouraged to hear what God has been teaching you and who can hold you accountable to what He spoke.

....
....
....

What steps of obedience or action steps are you going to take?

....
....
....

1. **Time and Place**—When and where did you meet with God?

....

....

....

2. **Be Still and Worship** (5–10 minutes)—Turn on worship music and ask God to help you connect to Him. Start by telling Him how wonderful He is and ask if there is any burden you need to release to Him. After you are finished, write down any impressions, thoughts, or themes you felt during your time of worship.

....

....

....

....

3. **Read and Pray** (10–15 minutes)—Read the following passage and use the SOAP method and the GOD SPA questions:

> "When Joseph's brothers saw that their father was dead, they said, 'What if Joseph holds a grudge against us and pays us back for all the wrongs we did to him?' So they sent word to Joseph, saying, 'Your father left these instructions before he died: "This is what you are to say to Joseph: I ask you to forgive your brothers the sins and the wrongs they committed in treating you so badly." Now please forgive the sins of the servants of the God of your father.' When their message came to him, Joseph wept. His brothers then came and threw themselves down before him. 'We are your slaves,' they said. But Joseph said to them, 'Don't be afraid. Am I in the place of God? You intended to harm me,

but God intended it for good to accomplish what is now being done, the saving of many lives. So then, don't be afraid. I will provide for you and your children.' And he reassured them and spoke kindly to them." (Genesis 50:15–21)

Observation—What stands out to you in this passage?

....

....

....

....

Application—How can you apply this passage to your life? (You may not have all of these answered for every passage, but it is helpful to ask the following questions.) Is there a/an:

Growth Area?

....

....

....

Obedience Needed?

....

....

....

Direction to Follow?

....

....

....

Sin to Confess?

....

....

....

Promise to Claim?

....

....

....

Accountability?

....

....

....

Prayer—Spend a minute in prayer asking God to help you apply these truths to your life.

4. **Write and Listen** (10–15 minutes)—Write a letter to God. This can be in response to what He was saying to you through Scripture or you can write Him about anything that is on your mind.

....

....

....

....

....

....

....

....

....

....

....

....

....

....

....

....

....

....

Listen for what God is saying to you. Write a letter to yourself from God with what you believe He is saying in response to you.

....
....
....
....
....
....
....
....
....
....
....
....
....
....
....

5. **Share and Obey** (After devo is completed)—With whom can you share what God spoke to you? If it is direction you received, it is wise to share this with the godly counsel in your life, and if it is revelation or insight, think about who would be encouraged to hear what God has been teaching you and who can hold you accountable to what He spoke.

....
....
....

What steps of obedience or action steps are you going to take?

....
....
....

Romans 12:1–10

1. **Time and Place**—When and where did you meet with God?

....

....

....

2. **Be Still and Worship** (5–10 minutes)—Turn on worship music and ask God to help you connect to Him. Start by telling Him how wonderful He is and ask if there is any burden you need to release to Him. After you are finished, write down any impressions, thoughts, or themes you felt during your time of worship.

....

....

....

3. **Read and Pray** (10–15 minutes)—Read the following passage and use the SOAP method and the GOD SPA questions:

> "Therefore, I urge you, brothers and sisters, in view of God's
> mercy, to offer your bodies as a living sacrifice, holy and pleas-
> ing to God—this is your true and proper worship. Do not con-
> form to the pattern of this world, but be transformed by the
> renewing of your mind. Then you will be able to test and ap-
> prove what God's will is—his good, pleasing and perfect will.
> For by the grace given me I say to every one of you: Do not
> think of yourself more highly than you ought, but rather think
> of yourself with sober judgment, in accordance with the faith
> God has distributed to each of you. For just as each of us has
> one body with many members, and these members do not all
> have the same function, so in Christ we, though many, form

one body, and each member belongs to all the others. We have different gifts, according to the grace given to each of us. If your gift is prophesying, then prophesy in accordance with your faith; if it is serving, then serve; if it is teaching, then teach; if it is to encourage, then give encouragement; if it is giving, then give generously; if it is to lead, do it diligently; if it is to show mercy, do it cheerfully. Love must be sincere. Hate what is evil; cling to what is good. Be devoted to one another in love. Honor one another above yourselves." (Romans 12:1–10)

Observation—What stands out to you in this passage?

....

....

....

....

Application—How can you apply this passage to your life? (You may not have all of these answered for every passage, but it is helpful to ask the following questions.) Is there a/an:

Growth Area?

....

....

....

Obedience Needed?

....

....

....

Direction to Follow?

....

....

....

Sin to Confess?

....
....
....

Promise to Claim?

....
....
....

Accountability?

....
....
....

Prayer—Spend a minute in prayer asking God to help you apply these truths to your life.

4. **Write and Listen** (10–15 minutes)—Write a letter to God. This can be in response to what He was saying to you through Scripture, or you can write Him about anything that is on your mind.

....
....
....
....
....
....
....
....
....
....
....
....

....

....

Listen for what God is saying to you. Write a letter to yourself from God
with what you believe He is saying in response to you.

....

....

....

....

....

....

....

....

....

....

....

....

5. **Share and Obey** (After devo is completed)—With whom can you
share what God spoke to you? If it is direction you received, it is wise to
share this with the godly counsel in your life, and if it is revelation or insight, think about who would be encouraged to hear what God has been
teaching you and who can hold you accountable to what He spoke.

....

....

....

What steps of obedience or action steps are you going to take?

....

....

....

Ezekiel 37:1–14

1. **Time and Place**—When and where did you meet with God?

....

....

....

2. **Be Still and Worship** (5–10 minutes)—Turn on worship music and ask God to help you connect to Him. Start by telling Him how wonderful He is and ask if there is any burden you need to release to Him. After you are finished, write down any impressions, thoughts, or themes you felt during your time of worship.

....

....

....

3. **Read and Pray** (10–15 minutes)—Read the following passage and use the SOAP method and the GOD SPA questions:

"The hand of the LORD was on me, and he brought me out by the Spirit of the LORD and set me in the middle of a valley; it was full of bones. He led me back and forth among them, and I saw a great many bones on the floor of the valley, bones that were very dry. He asked me, 'Son of man, can these bones live?' I said, 'Sovereign LORD, you alone know.' Then he said to me, 'Prophesy to these bones and say to them, 'Dry bones, hear the word of the LORD! This is what the Sovereign LORD says to these bones: I will make breath enter you, and you will come to life. I will attach tendons to you and make flesh come upon you and cover you with skin; I will put breath in you, and you will come to life. Then you will know that I am the LORD." So I prophesied

as I was commanded. And as I was prophesying, there was a noise, a rattling sound, and the bones came together, bone to bone. I looked, and tendons and flesh appeared on them and skin covered them, but there was no breath in them. Then he said to me, 'Prophesy to the breath; prophesy, son of man, and say to it, "This is what the Sovereign Lord says: Come, breath, from the four winds and breathe into these slain, that they may live."' So I prophesied as he commanded me, and breath entered them; they came to life and stood up on their feet—a vast army. Then he said to me: 'Son of man, these bones are the people of Israel. They say, 'Our bones are dried up and our hope is gone; we are cut off.' Therefore prophesy and say to them: "This is what the Sovereign Lord says: My people, I am going to open your graves and bring you up from them; I will bring you back to the land of Israel. Then you, my people, will know that I am the Lord, when I open your graves and bring you up from them. I will put my Spirit in you and you will live, and I will settle you in your own land. Then you will know that I the Lord have spoken, and I have done it, declares the Lord.'"
(Ezekiel 37:1–14)

Observation—What stands out to you in this passage?

....
....
....

Application—How can you apply this passage to your life? (You may not have all of these answered for every passage, but it is helpful to ask the following questions.) Is there a/an:

Growth Area?

....
....
....

Obedience Needed?

....
....
....

Direction to Follow?

....
....
....

Sin to Confess?

....
....
....

Promise to Claim?

....
....
....

Accountability?

....
....
....

Prayer—Spend a minute in prayer asking God to help you apply these truths to your life.

4. **Write and Listen** (10–15 minutes)—Write a letter to God. This can be in response to what He was saying to you through Scripture, or you can write Him about anything that is on your mind.

....
....

....
....
....
....
....
....
....
....
....
....
....
....
....
....

Listen for what God is saying to you. Write a letter to yourself from God with what you believe He is saying in response to you.

....
....
....
....
....
....
....
....
....
....
....
....
....
....
....
....

5. **Share and Obey** (After devo is completed)—With whom can you share what God spoke to you? If it is direction you received, it is wise to share this with the godly counsel in your life, and if it is revelation or insight, think about who would be encouraged to hear what God has been teaching you and who can hold you accountable to what He spoke.

....

....

....

What steps of obedience or action steps are you going to take?

....

....

....

2 Corinthians 4:7–18

1. **Time and Place**—When and where did you meet with God?

....

....

....

2. **Be Still and Worship** (5–10 minutes)—Turn on worship music and ask God to help you connect to Him. Start by telling Him how wonderful He is and ask if there is any burden you need to release to Him. After you are finished, write down any impressions, thoughts, or themes you felt during your time of worship.

....

....

....

3. **Read and Pray** (10–15 minutes)—Read the following passage and use the SOAP method and the GOD SPA questions:

> "But we have this treasure in jars of clay to show that this all-surpassing power is from God and not from us. We are hard pressed on every side, but not crushed; perplexed, but not in despair; persecuted, but not abandoned; struck down, but not destroyed. We always carry around in our body the death of Jesus, so that the life of Jesus may also be revealed in our body. For we who are alive are always being given over to death for Jesus' sake, so that his life may also be revealed in our mortal body. So then, death is at work in us, but life is at work in you. It is written: 'I believed; therefore I have spoken.' Since we have that same spirit of faith, we also believe and therefore speak, because we know that the one who raised the Lord Jesus from

the dead will also raise us with Jesus and present us with you to himself. All this is for your benefit, so that the grace that is reaching more and more people may cause thanksgiving to overflow to the glory of God. Therefore we do not lose heart. Though outwardly we are wasting away, yet inwardly we are being renewed day by day. For our light and momentary troubles are achieving for us an eternal glory that far outweighs them all. So we fix our eyes not on what is seen, but on what is unseen, since what is seen is temporary, but what is unseen is eternal." (2 Corinthians 4:7–18)

Observation—What stands out to you in this passage?

....
....
....

Application—How can you apply this passage to your life? (You may not have all of these answered for every passage, but it is helpful to ask the following questions.) Is there a/an:

Growth Area?

....
....
....

Obedience Needed?

....
....
....

Direction to Follow?

....
....
....

Sin to Confess?

....

....

....

Promise to Claim?

....

....

....

Accountability?

....

....

....

Prayer—Spend a minute in prayer asking God to help you apply these truths to your life.

4. **Write and Listen** (10–15 minutes)—Write a letter to God. This can be in response to what He was saying to you through Scripture, or you can write Him about anything that is on your mind.

....

....

....

....

....

....

....

....

....

....

....

....

Listen for what God is saying to you. Write a letter to yourself from God with what you believe He is saying in response to you.

....
....
....
....
....
....
....
....
....
....
....
....
....
....
....
....
....
....
....

5. **Share and Obey** (After devo is completed)—With whom can you share what God spoke to you? If it is direction you received, it is wise to share this with the godly counsel in your life, and if it is revelation or insight, think about who would be encouraged to hear what God has been teaching you and who can hold you accountable to what He spoke.

....
....
....

What steps of obedience or action steps are you going to take?

....
....
....

Matthew 20:1–16

1. **Time and Place**—When and where did you meet with God?

....
....
....

2. **Be Still and Worship** (5–10 minutes)—Turn on worship music and ask God to help you connect to Him. Start by telling Him how wonderful He is and ask if there is any burden you need to release to Him. After you are finished, write down any impressions, thoughts, or themes you felt during your time of worship.

....
....
....

3. **Read and Pray** (10–15 minutes)—Read the following passage and use the SOAP method and the GOD SPA questions:

> "For the kingdom of heaven is like a landowner who went out early in the morning to hire workers for his vineyard. He agreed to pay them a denarius for the day and sent them into his vineyard. About nine in the morning he went out and saw others standing in the marketplace doing nothing. He told them, 'You also go and work in my vineyard, and I will pay you whatever is right.' So they went. He went out again about noon and about three in the afternoon and did the same thing. About five in the afternoon he went out and found still others standing around. He asked them, 'Why have you been standing here all day long doing nothing?' 'Because no one has hired us,' they answered. He said to them, 'You also go and work in my vineyard.' When

evening came, the owner of the vineyard said to his foreman, 'Call the workers and pay them their wages, beginning with the last ones hired and going on to the first.' The workers who were hired about five in the afternoon came and each received a denarius. So when those came who were hired first, they expected to receive more. But each one of them also received a denarius. When they received it, they began to grumble against the landowner. 'These who were hired last worked only one hour,' they said, 'and you have made them equal to us who have borne the burden of the work and the heat of the day.' But he answered one of them, 'I am not being unfair to you, friend. Didn't you agree to work for a denarius? Take your pay and go. I want to give the one who was hired last the same as I gave you. Don't I have the right to do what I want with my own money? Or are you envious because I am generous?' So the last will be first, and the first will be last." (Matthew 20:1–16)

Observation—What stands out to you in this passage?

....

....

....

....

....

....

....

Application—How can you apply this passage to your life? (You may not have all of these answered for every passage, but it is helpful to ask the following questions.) Is there a/an:

Growth Area?

....

....

....

Obedience Needed?

....
....
....

Direction to Follow?

....
....
....

Sin to Confess?

....
....
....

Promise to Claim?

....
....
....

Accountability?

....
....
....

Prayer—Spend a minute in prayer asking God to help you apply these truths to your life.

4. **Write and Listen** (10–15 minutes)—Write a letter to God. This can be in response to what He was saying to you through Scripture, or you can write Him about anything that is on your mind.

....
....

....
....
....
....
....
....
....
....
....
....
....
....
....
....

Listen for what God is saying to you. Write a letter to yourself from God
with what you believe He is saying in response to you.

....
....
....
....
....
....
....
....
....
....
....
....
....
....
....
....
....
....

5. **Share and Obey** (After devo is completed)—With whom can you share what God spoke to you? If it is direction you received, it is wise to share this with the godly counsel in your life, and if it is revelation or insight, think about who would be encouraged to hear what God has been teaching you and who can hold you accountable to what He spoke.

....

....

....

What steps of obedience or action steps are you going to take?

....

....

....

1. **Time and Place**—When and where did you meet with God?

....

....

....

2. **Be Still and Worship** (5–10 minutes)—Turn on worship music and ask God to help you connect to Him. Start by telling Him how wonderful He is and ask if there is any burden you need to release to Him. After you are finished, write down any impressions, thoughts, or themes you felt during your time of worship.

....

....

....

3. **Read and Pray** (10–15 minutes)—Read the following passage and use the SOAP method and the GOD SPA questions:

> "Elijah went before the people and said, 'How long will you waver between two opinions? If the LORD is God, follow him; but if Baal is God, follow him.' But the people said nothing. Then Elijah said to them, 'I am the only one of the LORD's prophets left, but Baal has four hundred and fifty prophets. Get two bulls for us. Let Baal's prophets choose one for themselves, and let them cut it into pieces and put it on the wood but not set fire to it. I will prepare the other bull and put it on the wood but not set fire to it. Then you call on the name of your god, and I will call on the name of the LORD. The god who answers by fire—he is God.' Then all the people said, 'What you say is good.' Elijah said to the prophets of Baal, 'Choose one of the

bulls and prepare it first, since there are so many of you. Call on the name of your god, but do not light the fire.' So they took the bull given them and prepared it. Then they called on the name of Baal from morning till noon. 'Baal, answer us!' they shouted. But there was no response; no one answered. And they danced around the altar they had made. At noon Elijah began to taunt them. 'Shout louder!' he said. 'Surely he is a god! Perhaps he is deep in thought, or busy, or traveling. Maybe he is sleeping and must be awakened.' So they shouted louder and slashed themselves with swords and spears, as was their custom, until their blood flowed. Midday passed, and they continued their frantic prophesying until the time for the evening sacrifice. But there was no response, no one answered, no one paid attention. Then Elijah said to all the people, 'Come here to me.' They came to him, and he repaired the altar of the LORD, which had been torn down. Elijah took twelve stones, one for each of the tribes descended from Jacob, to whom the word of the LORD had come, saying, 'Your name shall be Israel.' With the stones he built an altar in the name of the LORD, and he dug a trench around it large enough to hold two seahs of seed. He arranged the wood, cut the bull into pieces and laid it on the wood. Then he said to them, 'Fill four large jars with water and pour it on the offering and on the wood.' 'Do it again,' he said, and they did it again. 'Do it a third time," he ordered, and they did it the third time. The water ran down around the altar and even filled the trench. At the time of sacrifice, the prophet Elijah stepped forward and prayed: 'LORD, the God of Abraham, Isaac and Israel, let it be known today that you are God in Israel and that I am your servant and have done all these things at your command. Answer me, LORD, answer me, so these people will know that you, LORD, are God, and that you are turning their hearts back again.' Then the fire of the LORD fell and burned up the sacrifice, the wood, the stones and the soil, and also licked up the water in the trench. When all the people saw this, they fell prostrate and cried, 'The LORD—he is God! The LORD—he is God!'" (I Kings 18:21–39)

Observation—What stands out to you in this passage?

....
....
....
....
....

Application—How can you apply this passage to your life? (You may not have all of these answered for every passage, but it is helpful to ask the following questions.) Is there a/an:

Growth Area?

....
....
....

Obedience Needed?

....
....
....

Direction to Follow?

....
....
....

Sin to Confess?

....
....
....

Promise to Claim?

....

....

....

Accountability?

....

....

....

Prayer—Spend a minute in prayer asking God to help you apply these truths to your life.

4. **Write and Listen** (10–15 minutes)—Write a letter to God. This can be in response to what He was saying to you through Scripture, or you can write Him about anything that is on your mind.

....

....

....

....

....

....

....

....

....

....

....

....

....

....

....

Listen for what God is saying to you. Write a letter to yourself from God with what you believe He is saying in response to you.

....
....
....
....
....
....
....
....
....
....
....
....
....
....
....

5. **Share and Obey** (After devo is completed)—With whom can you share what God spoke to you? If it is direction you received, it is wise to share this with the godly counsel in your life, and if it is revelation or insight, think about who would be encouraged to hear what God has been teaching you and who can hold you accountable to what He spoke.

....
....
....

What steps of obedience or action steps are you going to take?

....
....
....

John 13:1–16

1. Time and Place—When and where did you meet with God?

....

....

....

2. Be Still and Worship (5–10 minutes)—Turn on worship music and ask God to help you connect to Him. Start by telling Him how wonderful He is and ask if there is any burden you need to release to Him. After you are finished, write down any impressions, thoughts, or themes you felt during your time of worship.

....

....

....

3. Read and Pray (10–15 minutes)—Read the following passage and use the SOAP method and the GOD SPA questions:

> "It was just before the Passover Festival. Jesus knew that the hour had come for him to leave this world and go to the Father. Having loved his own who were in the world, he loved them to the end. The evening meal was in progress, and the devil had already prompted Judas, the son of Simon Iscariot, to betray Jesus. Jesus knew that the Father had put all things under his power, and that he had come from God and was returning to God; so he got up from the meal, took off his outer clothing, and wrapped a towel around his waist. After that, he poured water into a basin and began to wash his disciples' feet, drying them with the towel that was wrapped around him. He came to Simon Peter, who said to him, 'Lord, are you going to wash my

feet?' Jesus replied, 'You do not realize now what I am doing, but later you will understand.' 'No,' said Peter, 'you shall never wash my feet.' Jesus answered, 'Unless I wash you, you have no part with me.' 'Then, Lord,' Simon Peter replied, 'not just my feet but my hands and my head as well!' Jesus answered, 'Those who have had a bath need only to wash their feet; their whole body is clean. And you are clean, though not every one of you.' For he knew who was going to betray him, and that was why he said not every one was clean. When he had finished washing their feet, he put on his clothes and returned to his place. 'Do you understand what I have done for you?' he asked them. 'You call me "Teacher" and "Lord," and rightly so, for that is what I am. Now that I, your Lord and Teacher, have washed your feet, you also should wash one another's feet. I have set you an example that you should do as I have done for you. Very truly I tell you, no servant is greater than his master, nor is a messenger greater than the one who sent him.'" (John 13:1–16)

Observation—What stands out to you in this passage?

....
....
....
....
....
....

Application—How can you apply this passage to your life? (You may not have all of these answered for every passage, but it is helpful to ask the following questions.) Is there a/an:

Growth Area?

....
....
....

Obedience Needed?

....

....

....

Direction to Follow?

....

....

....

Sin to Confess?

....

....

....

Promise to Claim?

....

....

....

Accountability?

....

....

....

Prayer—Spend a minute in prayer asking God to help you apply these truths to your life.

4. **Write and Listen** (10–15 minutes)—Write a letter to God. This can be in response to what He was saying to you through Scripture, or you can write Him about anything that is on your mind.

....

....

....

....

....

....

....

....

....

....

....

....

....

....

....

....

Listen for what God is saying to you. Write a letter to yourself from God with what you believe He is saying in response to you.

....

....

....

....

....

....

....

....

....

....

....

....

....

....

....

....

5. **Share and Obey** (After devo is completed)—With whom can you share what God spoke to you? If it is direction you received, it is wise to share this with the godly counsel in your life, and if it is revelation or insight, think about who would be encouraged to hear what God has been teaching you and who can hold you accountable to what He spoke.

....

....

....

What steps of obedience or action steps are you going to take?

....

....

....

Daniel 3:13–29

1. **Time and Place**—When and where did you meet with God?

....
....
....

2. **Be Still and Worship** (5–10 minutes)—Turn on worship music and ask God to help you connect to Him. Start by telling Him how wonderful He is and ask if there is any burden you need to release to Him. After you are finished, write down any impressions, thoughts, or themes you felt during your time of worship.

....
....
....

3. **Read and Pray** (10–15 minutes)—Read the following passage and use the SOAP method and the GOD SPA questions:

> "Furious with rage, Nebuchadnezzar summoned Shadrach, Meshach and Abednego. So these men were brought before the king, and Nebuchadnezzar said to them, 'Is it true, Shadrach, Meshach and Abednego, that you do not serve my gods or worship the image of gold I have set up? Now when you hear the sound of the horn, flute, zither, lyre, harp, pipe and all kinds of music, if you are ready to fall down and worship the image I made, very good. But if you do not worship it, you will be thrown immediately into a blazing furnace. Then what god will be able to rescue you from my hand?' Shadrach, Meshach and Abednego replied to him, 'King Nebuchadnezzar, we do not need to defend ourselves before you in this matter. If we

are thrown into the blazing furnace, the God we serve is able to deliver us from it, and he will deliver us from Your Majesty's hand. But even if he does not, we want you to know, Your Majesty, that we will not serve your gods or worship the image of gold you have set up.' Then Nebuchadnezzar was furious with Shadrach, Meshach and Abednego, and his attitude toward them changed. He ordered the furnace heated seven times hotter than usual and commanded some of the strongest soldiers in his army to tie up Shadrach, Meshach and Abednego and throw them into the blazing furnace. So these men, wearing their robes, trousers, turbans and other clothes, were bound and thrown into the blazing furnace. The king's command was so urgent and the furnace so hot that the flames of the fire killed the soldiers who took up Shadrach, Meshach and Abednego, and these three men, firmly tied, fell into the blazing furnace. Then King Nebuchadnezzar leaped to his feet in amazement and asked his advisers, 'Weren't there three men that we tied up and threw into the fire?' They replied, 'Certainly, Your Majesty.' He said, 'Look! I see four men walking around in the fire, unbound and unharmed, and the fourth looks like a son of the gods.' Nebuchadnezzar then approached the opening of the blazing furnace and shouted, 'Shadrach, Meshach and Abednego, servants of the Most High God, come out! Come here!' So Shadrach, Meshach and Abednego came out of the fire, and the satraps, prefects, governors and royal advisers crowded around them. They saw that the fire had not harmed their bodies, nor was a hair of their heads singed; their robes were not scorched, and there was no smell of fire on them. Then Nebuchadnezzar said, 'Praise be to the God of Shadrach, Meshach and Abednego, who has sent his angel and rescued his servants! They trusted in him and defied the king's command and were willing to give up their lives rather than serve or worship any god except their own God. Therefore I decree that the people of any nation or language who say anything against the God of Shadrach, Meshach and Abednego be cut into pieces and their houses be turned into piles of rubble, for no other god can save in this way.' " (Daniel 3:13–29)

Observation—What stands out to you in this passage?

....
....
....
....
....

Application—How can you apply this passage to your life? (You may not have all of these answered for every passage, but it is helpful to ask the following questions.) Is there a/an:

Growth Area?

....
....
....

Obedience Needed?

....
....
....

Direction to Follow?

....
....
....

Sin to Confess?

....
....
....

Promise to Claim?

....

....

....

Accountability?

....

....

....

Prayer—Spend a minute in prayer asking God to help you apply these truths to your life.

4. **Write and Listen** (10–15 minutes)—Write a letter to God. This can be in response to what He was saying to you through Scripture, or you can write Him about anything that is on your mind.

....

....

....

....

....

....

....

....

....

....

....

....

....

....

....

....

....

Listen for what God is saying to you. Write a letter to yourself from God with what you believe He is saying in response to you.

....
....
....
....
....
....
....
....
....
....
....
....
....
....
....
....
....
....

5. **Share and Obey** (After devo is completed)—With whom can you share what God spoke to you? If it is direction you received, it is wise to share this with the godly counsel in your life, and if it is revelation or insight, think about who would be encouraged to hear what God has been teaching you and who can hold you accountable to what He spoke.

....
....
....

What steps of obedience or action steps are you going to take?

....
....
....

John 19:16–30

1. Time and Place—When and where did you meet with God?

....

....

....

2. Be Still and Worship (5–10 minutes)—Turn on worship music and ask God to help you connect to Him. Start by telling Him how wonderful He is and ask if there is any burden you need to release to Him. After you are finished, write down any impressions, thoughts, or themes you felt during your time of worship.

....

....

....

3. Read and Pray (10–15 minutes)—Read the following passage and use the SOAP method and the GOD SPA questions:

> "Finally Pilate handed him over to them to be crucified. So the soldiers took charge of Jesus. Carrying his own cross, he went out to the place of the Skull (which in Aramaic is called Golgotha). There they crucified him, and with him two others—one on each side and Jesus in the middle. Pilate had a notice prepared and fastened to the cross. It read: JESUS OF NAZARETH, THE KING OF THE JEWS. Many of the Jews read this sign, for the place where Jesus was crucified was near the city, and the sign was written in Aramaic, Latin and Greek. The chief priests of the Jews protested to Pilate, 'Do not write 'The King of the Jews,' but that this man claimed to be king of the Jews.' Pilate answered, 'What I have written, I have written.' When the sol-

diers crucified Jesus, they took his clothes, dividing them into four shares, one for each of them, with the undergarment remaining. This garment was seamless, woven in one piece from top to bottom. 'Let's not tear it,' they said to one another. 'Let's decide by lot who will get it.' This happened that the scripture might be fulfilled that said, 'They divided my clothes among them and cast lots for my garment.' So this is what the soldiers did. Near the cross of Jesus stood his mother, his mother's sister, Mary the wife of Clopas, and Mary Magdalene. When Jesus saw his mother there, and the disciple whom he loved standing nearby, he said to her, 'Woman, here is your son,' and to the disciple, 'Here is your mother.' From that time on, this disciple took her into his home. Later, knowing that everything had now been finished, and so that Scripture would be fulfilled, Jesus said, 'I am thirsty.' A jar of wine vinegar was there, so they soaked a sponge in it, put the sponge on a stalk of the hyssop plant, and lifted it to Jesus' lips. When he had received the drink, Jesus said, 'It is finished.' With that, he bowed his head and gave up his spirit." (John 19:16–30)

Observation—What stands out to you in this passage?

....
....
....
....

Application—How can you apply this passage to your life? (You may not have all of these answered for every passage, but it is helpful to ask the following questions.) Is there a/an:

Growth Area?

....
....
....

Obedience Needed?

....
....
....

Direction to Follow?

....
....
....

Sin to Confess?

....
....
....

Promise to Claim?

....
....
....

Accountability?

....
....
....

Prayer—Spend a minute in prayer asking God to help you apply these truths to your life.

4. **Write and Listen** (10–15 minutes)—Write a letter to God. This can be in response to what He was saying to you through Scripture, or you can write Him about anything that is on your mind.

....
....
....

....

....

....

....

....

....

....

....

....

....

....

....

....

....

Listen for what God is saying to you. Write a letter to yourself from God
with what you believe He is saying in response to you.

....

....

....

....

....

....

....

....

....

....

....

....

....

....

....

....

5. **Share and Obey** (After devo is completed)—With whom can you share what God spoke to you? If it is direction you received, it is wise to share this with the godly counsel in your life, and if it is revelation or insight, think about who would be encouraged to hear what God has been teaching you and who can hold you accountable to what He spoke.

....

....

....

What steps of obedience or action steps are you going to take?

....

....

....

1. **Time and Place**—When and where did you meet with God?

....

....

....

2. **Be Still and Worship** (5–10 minutes)—Turn on worship music and ask God to help you connect to Him. Start by telling Him how wonderful He is and ask if there is any burden you need to release to Him. After you are finished, write down any impressions, thoughts, or themes you felt during your time of worship.

....

....

....

3. **Read and Pray** (10–15 minutes)—Read the following passage and use the SOAP method and the GOD SPA questions:

> "The LORD said to Samuel, 'How long will you mourn for Saul, since I have rejected him as king over Israel? Fill your horn with oil and be on your way; I am sending you to Jesse of Bethlehem. I have chosen one of his sons to be king.' But Samuel said, 'How can I go? If Saul hears about it, he will kill me.' The LORD said, 'Take a heifer with you and say, 'I have come to sacrifice to the LORD.' Invite Jesse to the sacrifice, and I will show you what to do. You are to anoint for me the one I indicate.' Samuel did what the LORD said. When he arrived at Bethlehem, the elders of the town trembled when they met him. They asked, 'Do you come in peace?' Samuel replied, 'Yes, in peace; I have come to sacrifice to the LORD. Consecrate yourselves and come to the

sacrifice with me.' Then he consecrated Jesse and his sons and invited them to the sacrifice. When they arrived, Samuel saw Eliab and thought, 'Surely the LORD's anointed stands here before the LORD.' But the LORD said to Samuel, 'Do not consider his appearance or his height, for I have rejected him. The LORD does not look at the things people look at. People look at the outward appearance, but the LORD looks at the heart.' Then Jesse called Abinadab and had him pass in front of Samuel. But Samuel said, 'The LORD has not chosen this one either.' Jesse then had Shammah pass by, but Samuel said, 'Nor has the LORD chosen this one.' Jesse had seven of his sons pass before Samuel, but Samuel said to him, 'The LORD has not chosen these.' So he asked Jesse, 'Are these all the sons you have?' 'There is still the youngest,' Jesse answered. 'He is tending the sheep.' Samuel said, 'Send for him; we will not sit down until he arrives.' So he sent for him and had him brought in. He was glowing with health and had a fine appearance and handsome features. Then the LORD said, 'Rise and anoint him; this is the one.' So Samuel took the horn of oil and anointed him in the presence of his brothers, and from that day on the Spirit of the LORD came powerfully upon David. Samuel then went to Ramah." (I Samuel 16:1–13)

Observation—What stands out to you in this passage?

....

....

....

Application—How can you apply this passage to your life? (You may not have all of these answered for every passage, but it is helpful to ask the following questions.) Is there a/an:

Growth Area?

....

....

Obedience Needed?

....

....

Direction to Follow?

....

....

....

Sin to Confess?

....

....

Promise to Claim?

....

....

....

Accountability?

....

....

....

Prayer—Spend a minute in prayer asking God to help you apply these truths to your life.

4. **Write and Listen** (10–15 minutes)—Write a letter to God. This can be in response to what He was saying to you through Scripture, or you can write Him about anything that is on your mind.

....

....

....

....

....

....

....

....

....

....

....

....

....

....

....

....

Listen for what God is saying to you. Write a letter to yourself from God with what you believe He is saying in response to you.

....

....

....

....

....

....

....

....

....

....

....

....

....

....

....

....

....

5. **Share and Obey** (After devo is completed)—With whom can you share what God spoke to you? If it is direction you received, it is wise to share this with the godly counsel in your life, and if it is revelation or insight, think about who would be encouraged to hear what God has been teaching you and who can hold you accountable to what He spoke.

....

....

....

What steps of obedience or action steps are you going to take?

....

....

....

1. Time and Place—When and where did you meet with God?

....

....

....

2. Be Still and Worship (5–10 minutes)—Turn on worship music and ask God to help you connect to Him. Start by telling Him how wonderful He is and ask if there is any burden you need to release to Him. After you are finished, write down any impressions, thoughts, or themes you felt during your time of worship.

....

....

....

3. Read and Pray (10–15 minutes)—Read the following passage and use the SOAP method and the GOD SPA questions:

"After the Sabbath, at dawn on the first day of the week, Mary Magdalene and the other Mary went to look at the tomb. There was a violent earthquake, for an angel of the Lord came down from heaven and, going to the tomb, rolled back the stone and sat on it. His appearance was like lightning, and his clothes were white as snow. The guards were so afraid of him that they shook and became like dead men. The angel said to the women, 'Do not be afraid, for I know that you are looking for Jesus, who was crucified. He is not here; he has risen, just as he said. Come and see the place where he lay. Then go quickly and tell his disciples: 'He has risen from the dead and is going ahead of you into Galilee. There you will see him.' Now I have told you.' So the women hurried away from the tomb, afraid yet filled with joy, and ran to tell his disciples. Suddenly Jesus met them. 'Greetings,' he said. They came to him, clasped his feet and worshiped him. Then Jesus said to them, 'Do not be afraid. Go and tell my brothers to go to Galilee; there they will see me.' While the women were on their way, some of the guards went into the city and reported to the chief priests everything that had happened. When the chief priests had met with the elders and devised a plan, they gave the soldiers a large sum of money, telling them, 'You are to say, "His disciples came during the night and stole him away while we were asleep." If this report gets to the governor, we will satisfy him and keep you out of trouble.' So the soldiers took the money and did as they were instructed. And this story has been widely circulated among the Jews to this very day. Then the eleven disciples went to Galilee, to the mountain where Jesus had told them to go. When they saw him, they worshiped him; but some doubted. Then Jesus came to them and said, 'All authority in heaven and on earth has been given to me. Therefore go and make disciples of all nations, baptizing them in the name of the Father and of the Son and of the Holy Spirit, and teaching them to obey everything I have commanded you. And surely I am with you always, to the very end of the age.' " (Matthew 28:1–20)

Observation—What stands out to you in this passage?

....

....

....

....

....

....

....

....

Application—How can you apply this passage to your life? (You may not have all of these answered for every passage, but it is helpful to ask the following questions). Is there a/an:

Growth Area?

....

....

....

Obedience Needed?

....

....

....

Direction to Follow?

....

....

....

Sin to Confess?

....

....

....

Promise to Claim?

....

....

....

Accountability?

....

....

....

Prayer—Spend a minute in prayer asking God to help you apply these truths to your life.

4. **Write and Listen** (10–15 minutes)—Write a letter to God. This can be in response to what He was saying to you through Scripture, or you can write Him about anything that is on your mind.

....
....
....
....
....
....
....
....
....
....
....
....
....
....
....
....

Listen for what God is saying to you. Write a letter to yourself from God with what you believe He is saying in response to you.

....
....
....
....
....
....
....

....

....

....

....

....

....

....

....

....

....

5. **Share and Obey** (After devo is completed)—With whom can you share what God spoke to you? If it is direction you received, it is wise to share this with the godly counsel in your life, and if it is revelation or insight, think about who would be encouraged to hear what God has been teaching you and who can hold you accountable to what He spoke.

....

....

....

What steps of obedience or action steps are you going to take?

....

....

....

1. **Time and Place**—When and where did you meet with God?

....

....

....

2. **Be Still and Worship** (5–10 minutes)—Turn on worship music and ask God to help you connect to Him. Start by telling Him how wonderful He is and ask if there is any burden you need to release to Him. After you are finished, write down any impressions, thoughts, or themes you felt during your time of worship.

....

....

....

3. **Read and Pray** (10–15 minutes)—Read the following passage and use the SOAP method and the GOD SPA questions:

> "David asked, 'Is there anyone still left of the house of Saul to whom I can show kindness for Jonathan's sake?' Now there was a servant of Saul's household named Ziba. They summoned him to appear before David, and the king said to him, 'Are you Ziba?' 'At your service,' he replied. The king asked, 'Is there no one still alive from the house of Saul to whom I can show God's kindness?' Ziba answered the king, 'There is still a son of Jonathan; he is lame in both feet.' 'Where is he?' the king asked. Ziba answered, 'He is at the house of Makir son of Ammiel in Lo Debar.' So King David had him brought from Lo Debar, from the house of Makir son of Ammiel. When Mephibosheth son of Jonathan, the son of Saul, came to David, he

bowed down to pay him honor. David said, 'Mephibosheth!' 'At your service,' he replied. 'Don't be afraid,' David said to him, 'for I will surely show you kindness for the sake of your father Jonathan. I will restore to you all the land that belonged to your grandfather Saul, and you will always eat at my table.' Mephibosheth bowed down and said, 'What is your servant, that you should notice a dead dog like me?' Then the king summoned Ziba, Saul's steward, and said to him, 'I have given your master's grandson everything that belonged to Saul and his family. You and your sons and your servants are to farm the land for him and bring in the crops, so that your master's grandson may be provided for. And Mephibosheth, grandson of your master, will always eat at my table.' (Now Ziba had fifteen sons and twenty servants.) Then Ziba said to the king, 'Your servant will do whatever my lord the king commands his servant to do.' So Mephibosheth ate at David's table like one of the king's sons. Mephibosheth had a young son named Mika, and all the members of Ziba's household were servants of Mephibosheth. And Mephibosheth lived in Jerusalem, because he always ate at the king's table; he was lame in both feet." (2 Samuel 9:1–13)

Observation—What stands out to you in this passage?

....
....
....

Application—How can you apply this passage to your life? (You may not have all of these answered for every passage, but it is helpful to ask the following questions). Is there a/an:

Growth Area?

....
....
....

Obedience Needed?

....

....

....

Direction to Follow?

....

....

....

Sin to Confess?

....

....

....

Promise to Claim?

....

....

....

Accountability?

....

....

....

Prayer—Spend a minute in prayer asking God to help you apply these truths to your life.

4. **Write and Listen** (10–15 minutes)—Write a letter to God. This can be in response to what He was saying to you through Scripture or you can write Him about anything that is on your mind.

....

....

....

....

....

....

....

....

....

....

....

....

....

....

....

....

Listen for what God is saying to you. Write a letter to yourself from God with what you believe He is saying in response to you.

....

....

....

....

....

....

....

....

....

....

....

....

....

....

....

....

....

5. **Share and Obey** (After devo is completed)—With whom can you share what God spoke to you? If it is direction you received, it is wise to share this with the godly counsel in your life, and if it is revelation or insight, think about who would be encouraged to hear what God has been teaching you and who can hold you accountable to what He spoke.

....

....

....

What steps of obedience or action steps are you going to take?

....

....

....

Revelation 21:1–7

1. **Time and Place**—When and where did you meet with God?

....

....

....

2. **Be Still and Worship** (5–10 minutes)—Turn on worship music and ask God to help you connect to Him. Start by telling Him how wonderful He is and ask if there is any burden you need to release to Him. After you are finished, write down any impressions, thoughts, or themes you felt during your time of worship.

....

....

....

3. **Read and Pray** (10–15 minutes)—Read the following passage and use the SOAP method and the GOD SPA questions:

> "Then I saw 'a new heaven and a new earth,' for the first heaven and the first earth had passed away, and there was no longer any sea. I saw the Holy City, the new Jerusalem, coming down out of heaven from God, prepared as a bride beautifully dressed for her husband. And I heard a loud voice from the throne saying, 'Look! God's dwelling place is now among the people, and he will dwell with them. They will be his people, and God himself will be with them and be their God. He will wipe every tear from their eyes. There will be no more death or mourning or crying or pain, for the old order of things has passed away.' He who was seated on the throne said, 'I am making everything new!' Then he said, 'Write this down, for these words are trust-

worthy and true.' He said to me: 'It is done. I am the Alpha and the Omega, the Beginning and the End. To the thirsty I will give water without cost from the spring of the water of life. Those who are victorious will inherit all this, and I will be their God and they will be my children.'" (Revelation 21:1–7)

Observation—What stands out to you in this passage?

....

....

....

....

Application—How can you apply this passage to your life? (You may not have all of these answered for every passage, but it is helpful to ask the following questions.) Is there a/an:

Growth Area?

....

....

....

Obedience Needed?

....

....

....

Direction to Follow?

....

....

....

Sin to Confess?

....

....

....

Promise to Claim?

....

....

....

Accountability?

....

....

....

Prayer—Spend a minute in prayer asking God to help you apply these truths to your life.

4. **Write and Listen** (10–15 minutes)—Write a letter to God. This can be in response to what He was saying to you through Scripture, or you can write Him about anything that is on your mind.

....

....

....

....

....

....

....

....

....

....

....

....

....

....

....

....

....

Listen for what God is saying to you. Write a letter to yourself from God with what you believe He is saying in response to you.

....
....
....
....
....
....
....
....
....
....
....
....
....
....
....
....
....

5. **Share and Obey** (After devo is completed)—With whom can you share what God spoke to you? If it is direction you received, it is wise to share this with the godly counsel in your life, and if it is revelation or insight, think about who would be encouraged to hear what God has been teaching you and who can hold you accountable to what He spoke.

....
....
....

What steps of obedience or action steps are you going to take?

....
....
....

Acknowledgments

I would first and foremost like to thank **Jesus**. In the past twenty years of walking with You, I have learned there is no more worthwhile pursuit than knowing You and following Your voice. I am who I am because of You.

I would also like to thank:

Taryn—From the first time I met you and you told me that you wanted to "do something great for God," I knew you were the one I wanted with me on this journey. You have helped me become a better man, a better leader, and a better father. After fourteen years of marriage, I am even more in love with you, and I believe we are about to walk into our best season as we continue to follow God's voice together.

Isaac, Josiah, Asher, and Karis—I pray that you, too, will walk in this adventure of learning to hear and follow God's voice. You are my favorite legacy, and I can't wait to see what God does through each of your lives as you say yes to Him. I love you so much!

My parents—Dad, I watched you kneel beside your bed every night modeling a life of prayer, and, Mom, your love for God and for me helped me find Him. I would not be who I am today without both of your influences or the godly legacy you passed down to me.

My grandfather—I watched you study your Bible, while I studied your life, and you made me want to know the God that you knew. You taught me about hearing the voice of God and in many ways inspired the journey that led to this book. I can't wait to see you again.

Julie Reams—Thank you for all your help with every step of the journey toward my first book becoming published. You became my Baruch

(Jeremiah 36:32) as my scribe and editor, but, most important, as my friend. Your friendship is such a gift to Taryn and me.

Lisa Stilwell and the team at Howard Books—Thank you for believing in this message and for helping expand its reach. I appreciate your invaluable partnership.

Cassie Hanjian—Thank you for being an amazing literary agent and a champion for this message. I appreciate all your wisdom and help with the editing and publishing process.

DC Metro Launch Team—Thanks for following the voice of the Lord to embark upon the adventure of planting DC Metro Church with Taryn and me. We appreciate your support and belief in the vision before it was a reality more than you know.

DC Metro staff and family—We would not be where we are today if you had not chosen to invest your lives in this vision of building a God-first culture throughout the D.C. metro area. We are thankful for each of you, and we are excited to follow God's voice with you!

DC Metro Lead Team—It is an honor to do life and ministry with each of you. Leading the church with you has become a fun and fulfilling adventure. We are definitely better together.

Notes

Part One: Contact

1. "Americans Feel Connected to Jesus," Barna Group, published April 25, 2010, www.barna.org/barna-update/culture/364-americans-feel-connected-to-jesus#.Va_CtIr3anN.
2. Amos 3:7 (New King James Version).
3. Frank C. Laubach, *Channels of Spiritual Power* (New York: Fleming H. Revell Co., 1954), 92.
4. Exodus 29:42 (New Living Translation).
5. Lauren Morello, et al., "Obama Plays Scientific Favourites," *Nature*, April 11, 2013, www.nature.com/news/obama-plays-scientific-favourites-1.12787.
6. Albert Einstein quote, accessed April 7, 2016, www.quotes.net/quote/9306.

Part Two: The Practical Science of Hearing from God

Chapter One: Questions

1. Sylvia Earle quote, accessed October 20, 2014, www.brainyquote.com/quotes/authors/s/sylvia_earle.html.
2. Thomas Berger quote, retrieved October 20, 2014, www.brainyquote.com/quotes/authors/t/thomas_berger.html.
3. Philip Yancey, *Reaching for the Invisible God: What Can We Expect to Find?* (Grand Rapids, MI: Zondervan Publishing Company, 2000).
4. Timothy Keller quote, www.thegospelcoalition.org/article/20-quotes-from-tim-kellers-new-book-on-prayer.
5. Gerhard Freidrich, ed., *Theological Dictionary of the New Testament. vol. 5* (Grand Rapids: Wm. B. Eerdmans Publishing Company, 1967), 774–75.

6. Thoralf Gilbrant, ed., *The New Testament Greek-English Dictionary* (Springfield: The Complete Bible Library Co., 1986), 630.

7. Ibid., 385.

Chapter Two: Research

1. Albert Szent-Gyorgyi quote, http://thinkexist.com/quotes/albert_szent-gyorgyi/.

2. Carl Sagan quote, http://thinkexist.com/quotation/somewhere-something_incredible_is_waiting_to_be/154069.html.

3. 2 Timothy 2:15 (King James Version).

4. Ibid.

5. A. W. Tozer, *The Pursuit of God* (Harrisburg, PA: Christian Publications, 1948), 10.

6. Devotions & Journaling, www.enewhope.org/nextsteps/journaling/.

Chapter Three: Constructing and Testing the Hypothesis

1. Enrico Fermi quote, retrieved October 29, 2014, www.brainyquote.com/quotes/authors/e/enrico_fermi.html.

2. Proverbs 12:15 (New King James Version).

3. Proverbs 11:14 (New King James Version).

4. Peter Haas, Q&A, http://substancechurch.com/wp-content/uploads/2016/03/QA-ChurchSize2016.pdf.

5. *Forrest Gump*, directed by Robert Zemeckis, 1994, Paramount Pictures.

6. Larry Crabb, *The Safest Place on Earth*. (Nashville: Thomas Nelson Publishing, 1999), 22.

7. C. S. Lewis, *Letters to Malcolm: Chiefly on Prayer*. (New York: Harcourt, Brace & World, 1964), 93.

8. C. S. Lewis quote, www.goodreads.com/quotes/183419-in-friendship-we-think-we-have-chosen-our-peers-in-reality.

Chapter Four: Analysis and Conclusion

1. Milton Friedman quote, www.brainyquote.com/quotes/authors/m/milton_friedman.html#DQzdzAc8qgiLPLMf.99.

2. Thomas Edison quote, https://www.fi.edu/history-resources/edisons-light-bulb.

3. Joyce Bedi, "Thomas Edison's Inventive Life," published April 18, 2004, http://invention.si.edu/thomas-edisons-inventive-life.

4. "Edison's Lightbulb," www.fi.edu/history-resources/edisons-lightbulb.

5. Ibid.

6. William Barclay, *The New Daily Study Bible* (Louisville, KY:Westminster John Knox Press, 2004).

7. International Standard Bible Encyclopedia, www.studylight.org/encyclopedias/isb/.

8. Colossians 3:15 (New King James Version).

Chapter Five: Communicating Your Results

1. Revelation 19:10 (New King James Version).

Part Three: The Experiment— a 40-Day Guide to Hearing God's Voice

1. Psalm 32:8 (New King James Version).
2. 1 Kings 19:12 (King James Version).

About the Author

As Founding Pastor of DC Metro Church, Dr. David Stine is known for how he uses his practical biblical teaching, his visionary leadership, and his heart to impact the D.C. metropolitan area. David's authenticity and his ability to communicate the truth of God's Word in a humorous, dynamic, and revelatory manner helps people understand the Bible and how to apply its teachings to their everyday lives. David is passionate about people coming to know Christ, getting planted in God's house, and becoming transformational leaders who work together to build a God-first culture throughout the D.C. metro area and beyond.

Shortly after coming to Christ in college, David knew there was a call on his life to full-time ministry and sensed God leading him to seminary at Regent University, where he earned a Master of Practical Theology and a Doctorate of Ministry in Leadership. David met his future wife, Taryn, at Louisiana State University where they both majored in business and were involved in a campus ministry together. After graduation, they were advancing in their respective careers, but the deepest desire of their hearts was to do something great for God together. Today they are parents to four growing children and are loving their call to full-time ministry at DC Metro Church. They believe nothing compares to the joy of experiencing the transformation in people's lives as they choose the God-first life.

Contact the Author

If you have any comments or would like to share any way God has encouraged you or helped you grow in hearing His voice through reading this book, we would love to hear from you. You can contact David Stine at david@davidstine.com or by visiting davidstine.com/contact.

READING GROUP GUIDE

HEARING FROM
GOD

DAVID STINE

Study Guide Questions

Use these study guide questions to further personalize your study on *Hearing from God*. These questions can also be used to facilitate discussion in a small group, Bible study, or classroom environment.

1. We are all in different places in our journey in hearing from God. Where would you say that you are in learning to recognize His voice, His guidance, His direction? What helps you to recognize God's voice in your life?

2. What are the biggest hindrances in your life to having a regular devotional time with God, and what can you do to overcome these over the next twenty-one days?

3. Has God's voice guided you in any of the different ways that His voice can be heard? In the book, I shared six different ways that God's voice can be heard. They include: 1) Strong recurring thought; 2) Idea with genuine excitement; 3) Deep calming peace; 4) Inner warning, caution, or check; 5) Supernatural knowing; 6) Open/closed door. Of these six, which ways has God's voice guided you?

4. God's voice did not always come in dramatic audible manifestations throughout the Bible, but, instead, He was often heard as a still small voice. Why do you think this is how God frequently speaks?

5. In the event that our life gets off course, God is faithful in helping us quickly get back on track as long as we surrender to Him. Have you ever experienced this before?

6. How has God guided you through His Word? Can you think of a particular instance that He has spoken to you in His Word?

7. What makes you feel closer to God when studying His Word?

8. What is challenging for you about studying God's Word?

9. How has God's Word encouraged, directed, or corrected you recently?

10. How has God guided you through others? List some of the people that God has used most significantly in your life to guide you. Next to each person that you list, note how they have helped you.

11. Oftentimes God does not just put people into our lives to help us— He puts people in our lives for us to help them in His plan for their

lives. Using the same list from question 10, note next to each person how you can be an encouragement in her or his life.

12. In the book, I talk about having at least three **SAFE** (**S**upportive, **A**ccountable, **F**un, **E**mpowering), close Christian friends. Who is currently playing this role in your life? If you don't have three people yet, what are some ways you can be intentional in trying to find and develop these types of relationships?

13. How can you navigate relationships when you have a difference of opinion with someone who is a close friend or someone who is playing the role of godly counsel in your life?

14. Do you have any friendships or close relationships that have been through seasons of hurt, offense, or disagreement? Did you eventually reconcile with these people? How can you determine which relationships are worth fighting to keep and which relationships need to transition to a less central role in your life?

15. How can you keep your friendships healthy, growing, and encouraging so that you can be a conduit for God to speak through and encourage others through godly counsel?

16. We all struggle with peace from time to time. Do you feel like His peace is something that you struggle to have in your own life on a regular basis? What causes you to go without God's peace in your life most often?

17. How can you continue to position yourself for growth and hearing God's voice more clearly in the future?